Psychiatı ,
and the
Spirit World

"Beautifully written and meticulously researched, psychiatrist Alan Sanderson shares the journey to his ultimate understanding that we survive death of the physical body. He takes you by the hand and introduces you in a clear, sometimes humorous, way to various subjects proving this. This is a brilliant book by a caring physician. It is a book for everyone, no matter his or her religion, current beliefs, or even knowledge of the subject."

EDITH FIORE, PH.D., RETIRED CLINICAL PSYCHOLOGIST
AND AUTHOR OF *YOU HAVE BEEN HERE BEFORE:
A PSYCHOLOGIST LOOKS AT PAST LIVES*

"Fear of death and the belief that death is the end of consciousness is the greatest neurosis of humanity—a neurosis that has caused and still causes immense and unnecessary suffering. This book has one crucially important message for all of us: we survive death; the body dies but consciousness, or what used to be called the soul, survives; consciousness does not begin and end with the physical brain. The firewall erected between the visible and invisible dimensions of our experience—a firewall created by materialist or physicalist science—tells us that the universe is dead, the soul does not exist, and life has no transcendent meaning. This book offers a welcome release from our imprisonment in these limited beliefs and breaks the spell created by them. We are free to welcome and explore the many anomalous experiences dismissed for centuries by both science and religion. In this anxious time of living through a pandemic, when so many people are dying, this book will bring comfort and reassurance that there is life beyond the death of the body. We owe Alan Sanderson an immense debt of gratitude."

ANNE BARING, AUTHOR OF THE DREAM OF
THE COSMOS: A QUEST FOR THE SOUL

"I read Dr. Sanderson's *Psychiatry and the Spirit World* with fascination. He has brought together the full range of paranormal psychiatric techniques for curing mental illness. He specializes in spirit release, a therapy that brings healing to the victim by sending the attached or possessing spirit to the light. Using hypnosis, he engages the enraged, confused, or vengeful spirit and frees it. Dr. Sanderson laments that these highly successful techniques are never mentioned in medical schools and are shunned by most practicing psychiatrists, with their patients suffering the loss. The book also engagingly surveys much of the best research pointing to an afterlife. All told, *Psychiatry and the Spirit World* is a treasure for anyone bold enough to look for a fuller, more beneficial truth beyond the suffocating boundaries of an exclusively materialist science."

STAFFORD BETTY, PH.D., AUTHOR OF THE AFTERLIFE
THERAPIST AND THE AFTERLIFE UNVEILED

"Can you imagine a psychiatrist who has discovered the spirit world—and found it so valid and so helpful—that it is now a truth used in treatment? Prepare yourself. Miracles follow!"

P.M.H. ATWATER, L.H.D., RESEARCHER OF NEAR-DEATH
STATES FOR 42 YEARS AND AUTHOR OF THE FOREVER ANGELS:
NEAR-DEATH EXPERIENCES IN CHILDHOOD
AND THEIR LIFELONG IMPACT

Psychiatry

and the

Spirit World

True Stories on the
Survival of Consciousness
after Death

A Sacred Planet Book

ALAN SANDERSON, M.D., M.R.C.P., M.R.C.Psych.

Park Street Press
Rochester, Vermont

Park Street Press
One Park Street
Rochester, Vermont 05767
www.ParkStPress.com

Text stock is SFI certified

Park Street Press is a division of Inner Traditions International

Sacred Planet Books are curated by Richard Grossinger, Inner Traditions editorial board member and cofounder and former publisher of North Atlantic Books. The Sacred Planet collection, published under the umbrella of the Inner Traditions family of imprints, is comprised of works on the themes of consciousness, cosmology, alternative medicine, dreams, climate, permaculture, alchemy, shamanic studies, oracles, astrology, crystals, hyperobjects, locutions, and subtle bodies.

Cataloging-in-Publication Data for this title is available from the Library of Congress

ISBN 978-1-64411-576-3 (print)
ISBN 978-1-64411-577-0 (ebook)

Printed and bound in the United States by Lake Book Manufacturing, LLC. The text stock is SFI certified. The Sustainable Forestry Initiative® program promotes sustainable forest management.

10 9 8 7 6 5 4 3 2 1

Text design and layout by Virginia Scott Bowman
This book was typeset in Garamond Premier Pro and Legacy Sans with Acherus Grotesque and ArnoPro used as display typefaces

To send correspondence to the author of this book, mail a first-class letter to the author c/o Inner Traditions • Bear & Company, One Park Street, Rochester, VT 05767, and we will forward the communication, or contact the author directly at **Alan-Sanderson.com**.

♦♦♦

To my dearest Sophia, who supported
my writing wonderfully

New Way

These words ring out to you for your fresh thinking.
They'll bring fresh energy to all you do.
Open them wide and they will open you.

ALAN SANDERSON

Contents

Foreword

Most people fear dying, if they even allow themselves to consider their own deaths at all. They believe it's the absolute end. Some would explain it this way: "When you're dead, you're dead. That's it!" There are those who fear going to hell or hope that they are going to heaven. And how very scary to think of not being alive any longer! Can we even comprehend that?

That is why Alan Sanderson's book, *Psychiatry and the Spirit World,* is such an important and valuable contribution to our understanding about what really happens after the body dies. As you read, you will learn beyond a shadow of a doubt that the soul, you, continues uninterruptedly and always has.

Dr. Sanderson has drawn his conclusions from his experience as a practicing psychiatrist, eventually using hypnosis to access the subconscious mind, which is the storehouse of all memories of the current life and previous ones. He also used a very effective technique to find and release earthbound spirits who were harming his patients. In those cases, the actual patient was the spirit who, after their own death, became trapped in someone else's body and was not able to continue their own life in another realm to make spiritual progress.

He explains his evolution from a conventional doctor to one who went his own way and was able to help patients more effectively. At the same time, he learned that life does continue after death.

Besides being a clinician and healer, he is also a seeker of knowledge beyond the mainstream. So he shares with the reader fascinating topics related to a soul's survival after death and to other psychic phenomena. You will read about past lives, near-death experiences, and mediumship, which involves a living person communicating with someone who is in the spirit world.

Some of the topics will be familiar to you, and others may seem impossible, but Dr. Sanderson's accounts and the careful observations of many meticulous researchers will open your mind to new probabilities. For example, you will learn that the mind, or consciousness, can separate from the brain. It can rise above the body and observe the body below and can even travel and, in some documented instances, affect other people.

This is also the case in near-death experiences in which the body has died (and hence the brain has died) and later comes back to life. The person who died has a vivid memory of what happened before the body was revived.

Dr. Sanderson explains all of this in a kind, gentle manner. In the beginning of this book, he asks you to take his hand, and as you both explore the many topics, he talks to you, asks you questions, and even asks himself questions. It's as though you both are walking together through various rooms, each filled with a wonderful subject matter. You will feel you are with a lovely friend who is thrilled to share all those wonders with you. I found the book delightful to read because of Dr. Sanderson's being so personally present with me through the very interesting chapters.

A great many years of research went into the writing of his book. Besides the abundant number of accounts, Dr. Sanderson suggests other books, YouTube programs, and articles for you to further explore the various topics. It is a real education!

In many ways, Dr. Sanderson and I share a similar development. I didn't believe in reincarnation, knew nothing of possessing spirits, and also like most people assumed, if I even thought about it, that death was the end. However, while using regression hypnotic therapy, a patient of mine recalled what seemed like a past life and was relieved of a troubling symptom. Then there was another, also cured. They both believed in reincarnation; therefore, I discounted the validity of their experiences. However, a third patient was someone who didn't believe in past lives, as I didn't, and she also was cured. All three simply recalled their past lives, without my giving them any suggestions regarding their symptoms. That did it for me. I realized there was something important going on.

Then, what I thought were multiple personalities turned out to be other people inhabiting my patients' bodies. I learned a technique to help them leave, which resulted in instantaneous cures. So, as a result of treating thousands of patients successfully with these two modes of therapy, my worldview changed, and I came to believe that life does indeed continue after death. In fact, it's more than a belief. It's a knowing that we don't die; we live on in a different way.

As you can imagine, the information in Dr. Sanderson's book is totally compatible with my own knowledge and experience. By adding the work of others and including their many fascinating accounts, he is able to cover a field much wider than any single therapist could cover through personal experience alone. In this way, he is able to confirm my certainty of survival of bodily death with even greater conviction.

In my opinion, his book is a treasure.

EDITH FIORE, PH.D.,
RETIRED CLINICAL PSYCHOLOGIST

Edith Fiore, Ph.D., practiced in California for more than thirty years, first with a general clinical practice and then from 1975 on as a hypnotherapist. She retired in 1997 and now lives in Florida. She has lectured nationally and internationally and has trained more than two thousand professionals in her innovative techniques as a hypnotherapist. She is the author of *The Unquiet Dead: A Psychologist Treats Spirit Possession* and *You Have Been Here Before: A Psychologist Looks at Past Lives.*

Preface

Three times in my life, individuals scarcely known to me have made suggestions that, although I had no means of foretelling it, were to bring tremendous changes. The first occasion was in March 1958, when a dinner companion in Nairobi said that if he were a doctor in my situation, with some weeks to spend before returning home, he would visit Albert Schweitzer, recipient of the 1952 Nobel Peace Prize, whose jungle hospital in the Gabon was world-renowned. The idea had not occurred to me, but I thought, "Nothing ventured, nothing gained!" A few weeks later I went to Lambarene and met not only Dr. Schweitzer but my future wife and mother-to-be of our five children, Trudi Bochsler, who was in charge of Schweitzer's leper colony. What a life-changer!

The second big change was when a colleague, with whom I did volunteer work in a prison, put the I Ching, or Book of Changes, in my hands, saying, "I have two of these. This may interest you." The I Ching, the world's oldest oracle, was unknown to me then, but it became a powerful influence on my decisions, especially in writing this book.

Change number three came in 1992, when, within two years of returning to clinical psychiatry, I undertook a research project on eye-movement desensitization, a treatment for phobic states. A research volunteer advised me to meet Lance Trendall, a hypnotherapist. Lance introduced me to spirit attachment as a cause of psychiatric disturbance.

Working with attached spirits was an unknown area for me, but it made a tremendous contribution to my treatment approach, as you will learn.

I trained in hypnosis and spirit release in the United Kingdom and America. Soon I was using these techniques with my National Health Service (NHS) patients in Fairfield Hospital and at the Leighton Buzzard Psychiatric Clinic. The treatment proved highly successful, and I used it for some years before the NHS decided that, as spirit release was not an officially approved treatment, its use was inappropriate. After leaving the NHS, it was a simple matter to continue to use spirit release privately, and I founded the Spirit Release Foundation in 1999, as I discuss in the introduction.

The last of my three life-changing decisions profoundly affected my working life and will, I hope, affect the lives of many others who read this book. To write a book about my experience seemed a natural choice, but writing about spirit release as a form of psychiatric practice would have required hospital resources that were not available to me. So I chose the alternative, which was to write for a general readership on a wider subject, focusing especially on survival after bodily death.

Writing for you, I feel like a brimstone, England's first spring butterfly, with its pale butter-colored wings, racing over the fields and woodland, on its mission of deliverance from chill winds and an unforgiving winter. Now I'm on a flight of adventure, and you're with me as a traveling companion, off to discover new things and old, new thoughts and new ways!

My best thought is simply to take your hand and show you what happened when I treated my patients for troublesome spirits. The presence of spirits in patients was totally unexpected, but what a wonderful find! To my delight, I learned how to benefit those who were in such trouble. This knowledge completely contradicted my medical training. I lacked the power to influence the traditional methods of treatment, but on retiring from clinical work, I was free to write for everyone with the good fortune to share my interests.

This book has one tremendous aim: to demonstrate that death is not the end. Every religion teaches survival of physical death, but my belief has not come from religion. Religion does not provide proof and is not interested in research, whereas for me research and proof are essential. And research has been building, particularly during the past sixty years, and has reached the state where we can now be certain that we survive physical death.

The book also speaks for all those who find today's scientific world-view limiting because it fails to meet our deepest needs, in particular the need to know that life has meaning. The problem with conventional science is that it is limited by the philosophy of materialism, or physical-ism, as it is now often named,* which acknowledges only features perceived by biological perceptual processes or their technical replacements and maintains that no living activity occurs outside the constraints of physical existence. Today's science will not even look at phenomena outside this very restricted area, which means that the spiritual domain is denied and excluded from consideration. However, these hidden ways do exist, and they have tremendous implications for our lives, generally, and for our existence beyond bodily life.

I cannot give you a direct awareness of what I experienced, but I can tell you about it and give you my thoughts and examples. Relating an experience, though, however intense, cannot approach the impact of having it in person. How should I bring it alive for you? I shall describe a few of my own experiences with patients and add many related experiences as told by others. In the following pages, I shall relate two sorts of evidence: direct and indirect. Direct accounts are concerned with survival of physical death, and indirect accounts are concerned with disproving the philosophy of physicalism, on which contemporary science depends.

That, in broad outline, is my plan: to provide many great stories from me and others. The word *story* has often been used to describe

---

*To avoid confusion with the definition of *materialism* as "the importance of material possessions over spiritual values," the term will hereafter be replaced by *physicalism*.

creative works, but my stories result from keen observation and are instances of sound evidence that cover the wide range of necessary research. In addition, the transcribed accounts are told in a variety of writing styles, which makes reading more interesting.

Much has changed since I began writing eight years ago. More than ever, the world is in turmoil, crying out for help. Climatic changes are having devastating effects, which seem certain to get worse. Political and economic crises abound. Few of us are able to contribute to a solution, but we can all change ourselves. We shall then be in a much better state to manage the difficulties and to develop our lives more fully. That, alone, will be a great contribution. I believe that, in this time of crisis, how we live individually and together is all-important. This book is a preparation for essential change. It will bring copious information to your attention and stimulate new thoughts. I should like to feel that I can talk to you as a valued companion on our journey through the land of questions.

I intend to inform as many people as possible of the full force of events. In addition, it is important to stress the very serious misinformation to which science, education, medical practice, advertising, and the media are subjecting us on the matter of after-death survival. We do survive. That is the essential truth. However, it is hard work getting this message across the blockage from official sources.

Thousands of books have been written about psychic phenomena. Why write another?

My reasons are as follows:

- There is convincing evidence that physical death is simply a changing state, not permanent extinction.
- This vastly complex realm needs to be widely known and publicized.
- Although ignored by contemporary science and medicine, there is no recent publication that includes the whole area of psychic experience in light of current research.

- It is time for an update of this highly important subject to be represented to the general reader in a way that is easy to follow.
- In the experience of many doctors and non-doctors, spirit release is a highly effective treatment in many cases of spirit attachment. This has yet to be officially investigated and publicized.

Many will think that in writing about this largely unknown and vastly complex area in one small book, I am taking on an impossible task. I can only respond by asking, Can there be anything more fascinating and more necessary?

Revolutionary Introduction

Truth is often hidden by fear, fear of the unknown and fear of being laughed at for accepting observations outside the doctrine of conventional belief.

Children may put adults on the spot with questions about the afterlife, for which they are poorly prepared. Here is my fantasied example in which little Lewis gets his uncles arguing:

LEWIS: What happens when we die? What is Heaven like and how do I get there? Is Granny there, waiting for me?

MARK: Lewis, your questions never stop! Give us a break, lad!

JOE: What do you expect, Mark? Young Lewis is only six. He has to learn. In a way he's teaching us.

MARK: Teaching us? That's a good one. What must we learn, then?

JOE: Lewis teaches us to keep questioning. When we grow up, the questions fade away. We just stop thinking.

MARK: Stop thinking? Come on, that's rubbish!

JOE: Oh no, it's not! Most of us stop thinking creatively.

MARK: What would you do about it, then?

JOE: Listen to this account of an event that happened in 1887:

The Find

A normal day on the farm. The silver watch and chain of Wesley Davis, a young laborer in Vermont, USA, were his prized possessions.

1

Wesley spent the day alone, mending the fence around a remote pasture. It was a long, long day. And at the end of that day, he discovered that his watch had gone. Disappeared. He had no idea how it had happened. What a disaster!

Wesley's friend John was as upset as he was. Even three days later, John was still troubled. That night he dreamed of Wesley's watch. He saw watch and chain lying where they had fallen. They were in an area where John had never been, but rocks, trees and the surroundings were perfectly plain to him. The others laughed when he told them at breakfast. Unaffected by their derision, John saddled a horse and rode to the field. And there was the watch, located exactly as in his dream.

The farmer was so impressed that he sent the account to Professor William James, a renowned philosopher, psychologist, and medical doctor.[1]

The account, as named and written here, gives my idea of what may actually have been sent to Dr. James. So, how have I come to write this for you? I'll start with my formative experiences.

FORMATIVE EXPERIENCES

It's 1941. Boys are walking around the Triangle, an open space at Sandroyd School, where we had been evacuated to avoid the London Blitz. My neighbor, another ten-year-old, had a tummy ache and asked me what to do. Goodness knows what I told him, but later that day his tummy and I had both found happiness: the ache was gone, and I had decided to be a doctor. Where the decision came from, goodness knows, but by 1948 I was in medical school, pursuing my planned path. There was just one competing subject: psychic phenomena.

My mother, who died in a riding accident in 1940, may have influenced me in this. Exploring a bookshelf in her bedroom, I found some books on spiritual matters, including Paul Brunton's *A Search in Secret Egypt* and Maurice Maeterlinck's *The Unknown Guest*. Their accounts thrilled and intrigued me. I visited Foyles bookshop, where the second-hand department had a few books on such topics. There I found J. W. Dunne's *An Experiment with Time* and other treasures. I remember how in 1949, on family holiday, I told my father that, on qualification, I would commit my life to research on psychic experience. He was horrified. "Don't let me ever hear you say that again." He never did. However, my interest in psychic experience didn't go away; it found expression in psychiatry.

DECADES OF RESEARCH

After my training in psychiatry, I researched the connection between facial structure and personality, which, while not in the psychic category, was far from accepted belief. It was a fascinating study, with considerable potential for extending knowledge of the genetics of personality, but after two decades, I finally had to accept that my study could not succeed with my computer technology skills and statistical expertise at such a low level.

RETURN TO CLINICAL PSYCHIATRY

With Trudi's persuasion, I returned to clinical psychiatry. Not much had changed in clinical practice, but I found the experience of again working with patients in a clinical setting a great joy. As a consultant psychiatrist at Fairfield Hospital, not far from London, I initiated a research project into eye-movement desensitization, a treatment for post-traumatic stress disorder, which, as I mentioned in the preface, led to a meeting with Lance Trendall, a hypnotist who was using a technique to release spirits who had attached themselves to living individuals.

SPIRIT RELEASE–MY LIFE'S WORK

This was as far from conventional psychiatry as cricket is from cookery. Could there be something to it? I was intrigued. Medical literature informed me that I was by no means the first therapist on this path. Lance gave me two books on the subject—one by psychiatrist Carl Wickland and the other by psychologist Edith Fiore—each of which described very different approaches. Both therapists had great success in freeing patients from intrusive spirits. Dr. Fiore, whom we shall meet again, used hypnosis. With her patients in trance, she conversed with spiritual presences, persuading them to leave. Her two-way communication appealed to me. Encouraged by what I read, I invited Lance to Fairfield, where I could observe his simpler approach with my patients, several of whom gladly accepted the offer of hypnotherapy.

Lance quickly had his subjects in trance. He then addressed whatever troublesome symptom the patient had complained of, whether anger, depression, anxiety, inner voice, and so on, asking it to sit on the empty chair beside him. When the patient had left, Lance turned to the chair and spoke to the presumed spirit, encouraging it to go to the Light, where it would find a deceased relative or spirit guide. While Lance's method lacked the adaptability of Fiore's dialogue, some patients derived definite benefit. Paul, a lad of nineteen, had been admitted after a serious suicide attempt. He was bombarded by voices, but a maximal dose of antipsychotic medication was entirely ineffective. Normally a gentle lad, he attempted to strangle a nurse and was placed on close observation. We had no more medical interventions to offer.

Paul's parents readily accepted my offer of hypnosis with Lance, and Paul agreed. Lance induced trance and spoke to the presumed spirits, asking them to leave. After some minutes, Paul opened his eyes and said, "They've gone." For several days, the voices stopped completely. When they returned, they were fainter and ineffective. Paul's dangerous behavior did not return. This response amazed me. Paul's behavior had been floridly psychotic and out of control but had responded to hypnosis with Lance. I had to build on this.

Paul's response was a eureka experience. How it worked was unclear, but I took it as an indication that spirits were involved in Paul's condition. It was only one case, but it confirmed Wickland's and Fiore's findings.

Hypnosis and Spirit Release Training

I trained in hypnosis and went to Florida in 1993 for a weeklong course with William Baldwin, the world leader in spirit release training. In 1994, I cautiously introduced spirit release into my clinical practice. I was careful not to suggest to my National Health Service (NHS) patients that hypnosis could lead to a spiritual experience.

Spirit Release for National Health Service Patients

I simply said that it might bring a helpful connection to the unconscious mind. I used techniques such as having my entranced patient look at an imaginary mirror. If they described either a change in bodily appearance or the image of another person, I would try to obtain a response by voice or yes-no finger signals. If the response indicated an attached spirit, I encouraged it to leave. Sometimes this was successful, and the effect lasted. Of course, I couldn't know if it would be permanent, and there was no certainty that I was dealing with spirits. This was pioneering work. The search for understanding, desirable as that achievement may be, can so easily hold back a promising treatment. Advances need chances.

It was exciting to be working in a way that gave such tremendous opportunities for therapeutic progress. I longed to discuss my experience with colleagues, but we worked in different worlds. With my new treatment I felt like a desert explorer, where unknown exotic plants were dying of drought. I had a source of water but only a thimble in which to carry it. If others learned what I was doing, my thimble might be taken away and the plants would die.

Although I asked patients not to discuss their treatment, they often lost no time in sharing experiences with other patients on the ward. Some staff members were unhappy about the treatment, which I had not felt able to discuss with them. As they saw it, I was practicing "voodoo." This difficult situation affected all of us. Hospital managers were concerned. I invited my senior psychiatric colleague and the chief executive of the hospital trust to attend treatment sessions with patients. Although they expressed interest, the end came when the official purchasing authority declined to purchase the treatment on the grounds that it was not in general use—scarcely an encouraging attitude for researchers.

NHS Bans Spirit Release

I was asked to give an account of my work to the trust management committee. They decided that spirit release therapy must not be given to NHS patients. I was forbidden to treat even my private patients on NHS premises. Official wheels had taken time to turn, and I had been using spirit release and past-life therapy with considerable success for a couple of years, on perhaps fifty patients. With this experience, I was well prepared to offer spirit release privately.

After leaving the NHS in 1997, it was a relief to state freely that I was specializing in spiritually based treatment. In 1999, after giving a lecture on spirit attachment to the College of Psychic Studies, London, I was encouraged by members of the audience to found a nonmedical organization to support and encourage therapists who had an interest in the subject.

Spirit Release Foundation 1999–2012

My time with the Spirit Release Foundation, first as chair and later as president, was enjoyable and formative. The experience of using spirit release with a wide range of patients and working with a varied group of nonmedical therapists using many different methods was invaluable, helping both patients and therapists. However, after twelve years, the foundation was in financial difficulties, and a new organization, the nonmedical Spirit Release Forum, organized on commercial lines, took on the work.

MY BOOK

Having retired from clinical work, it was inconceivable for me to sink into inactivity. I was not in a position to promote my views on psychiatric practice, but there was one highly important matter open to me. I could write about my views for a nonmedical audience. I would focus on the spiritual dimension as it affects members of the public, particularly on the subject of survival after physical death. This is an essential matter for many people because so much depends on it. I have written for those who long for reliable information about the spirit world. In particular, I have tried to use a style that makes the book widely accessible to the general public. My hope is that people will read a few pages, just for the joy of it, and perhaps pass a story on to friends or family as something to wonder at. I also hope that therapists who are open to psychic experience, apart from religious teaching, will find my book of value for their work.

THE IMPORTANCE OF A WORLDVIEW

In ancient times, Babylonians would lie on the desert sand and gaze at the night sky, wondering about the stars and asking themselves where answers might be found. There are many spiritual questions to answer: Where do I fit in? Does life have a purpose? Why are we here? How should we behave? What is the soul? What happens after we die? What meaning have the lives that we live in this extraordinary world and beyond?

Science tells us that life has no purpose and that all life, mankind included, has occurred by chance. Science has been so successful that we tend to think that it must know best on everything. Even so, when we see that science rejects everything that cannot be measured or sensed by our five organs of perception, we have to wonder.

SCIENCE AND PHYSICALISM

The philosophy of physicalism, as described earlier in the preface, is mere surmise, yet science clings to this unproven conjecture and uses it to dismiss, without scrutiny, all spiritual beliefs, even though they are held by millions.

It is also important to remind ourselves that Western science is very much alone in this view. Every religion, the world over, believes that life continues beyond physical death, yet science holds that there is no soul, consciousness is entirely dependent on the brain, and brain death is the end of consciousness. Science is certain about this. Isn't that extraordinary? How could applying the scientific system of careful observation, hypothesis formation, measurement, and recording result in a statement of such certainty? It could happen only because science has embraced physicalism, without the necessary consideration of the many anomalies that don't fit into such a limited worldview. The chief reason physicalist scientists give for this limited worldview is that because consciousness seems not to survive the certainty of brain death, the brain must produce consciousness. This is the immediate impression, but it is contradicted by many other findings, notably:

1. Near-death experience, in which the subject later gives veridical evidence of consciousness by telling of observations, at a distance, that are later confirmed
2. Reincarnation in very young children, of which there is much evidence in chapter 9
3. Predictive mediumship

Worldview is an important concept, and we need to give the matter careful thought. It is not enough to repeat the views of others unless we understand them fully. We need our own dependable worldview to guide us in our choices. And while respecting the worldviews of others is a positive attitude to take, it does not mean that two conflicting worldviews can both be true in the absolute sense. And yet, we cannot prove worldviews one way or the other—not yet. Of course, not all conceivable worldviews are reasonable. Take, for instance, the view that the world is flat. That view goes right against the observed evidence. We have seen well-authenticated pictures of our world from space, and we know it is as round as an orange.

As we continue to become more informed about the world around us, our views will change, but I am expecting that we shall still hold a range of thoughtful beliefs. I must hope that, by the end of the book, it will be possible for all readers to express a considered worldview.

Science has developed such impressive knowledge and so many

powerful and profitable technologies that it has assumed the position of supreme authority, a situation that is usually unquestioned by government, industry, education, and the media. This book equips you to ask relevant questions based on observations of actual events rather than theories.

ANOMALOUS EVENTS

We'll start by focusing on what science calls anomalous events. An anomaly is a finding that cannot be explained within the current scientific concept. Innumerable such events have been recorded by organizations such as the Institute of Noetic Sciences, or IONS in the United States and the Scientific and Medical Network, the College of Psychic Studies, and the Society for Psychical Research in the United Kingdom. Beneath the surface, there are countless numbers of anomalous experiences suppressed by experiencers for fear of derision. Here, in coming chapters, you will find a wealth of anomalies taken from the literature. Each of them is relevant to the big question: What happens when we die?

As mentioned in the preface, in considering this question, it seems simplest to divide examples into two categories: direct and indirect. Direct topics are specifically related to dying. Examples include end-of-life experiences, near-death experiences, reincarnation, mediumship, and spirit attachment. Indirect topics, while not directly related to dying, are important because they challenge scientific physicalism. The predictive dream in the story "The Find," told at the beginning of this introduction, is an example of an indirect topic.

"The Find" is a fascinating account, but as always, detractors will raise the problem of authenticity. Is it fact or fabrication? At this distance there can be no certainty. Since this question will be with us throughout the book, we'll consider it now.

Most scientists and members of the Skeptics Society (not my favorite organization) will instantly dismiss or ignore anything that falls outside preconceived beliefs. The Skeptics Society was founded in the United

States in 1992 and, on the basis of journal sales, claims fifty thousand members. Those members, called "organized skeptics," are unusual folk, for they've assumed a social obligation to protect the general population from any practice (organized religion excluded), anomaly, or anecdote that has a spiritual or psychic nature, or what they call "pseudoscience," which means nonphysicalist science.

ANECDOTES

My view is that anecdotal accounts should be rejected only when there are powerful reasons for suspicion. The word *anecdotal* comes from the Greek *anekdota*, meaning unpublished, but for scientists it has come to mean an individual experience that cannot be put to the usual scientific tests, and in particular, repeatability. There is scarcely one anecdote of any nature that cannot be dismissed if one goes to extreme lengths in assuming dishonesty. In "The Find," we might suppose that John had stolen his friend's watch and then thought better of it and decided to return it. He could have made up the dream and created the story as told. It seems unlikely, but one cannot deny the possibility. Let's suppose we have a hundred accounts of dreams accurately foretelling events. Would possible dishonesty by reporters be a valid cause for dismissing the lot? Such a course cannot be justified unless the theory of physicalism were to be proved beyond question—an impossibility, with so many questions still unanswered. Physicalism cannot be proved. Despite this, proof is invariably assumed by physicalist scientists. This leads to automatic dismissal of psychic events.

In defense of anecdotal accounts, the bundle-of-sticks metaphor is being offered. One stick can be easily broken, but breaking a bundle may require superhuman strength. For these reasons I accept the watch dream. It is one of a great many related accounts, which adds significantly to its strength.

If precognition, telepathy, psychokinesis, or clairvoyance were proven with just one certain case, it would require major changes in scientific theory. Many scientists would be horrified at this prospect, as it would mean that they might see something that would threaten their physical-ist worldview.

GALILEO

We need a word about Galileo here. He is often held up as an example of an explorer who got into trouble because the Church could not tol-erate his observation-based conclusion that the Earth is not the center of the Universe. (He was not the first, of course, but Copernicus and Kepler had no telescopes.) It was the observational evidence that caused the trouble. Galileo's telescope revealed Jupiter's moons, which accord-ing to the Christian story could not exist. The churchmen refused to use the telescope. Scientists who refuse to examine evidence for telepa-thy because they consider it impossible can be likened to the churchmen of the 1660s. It's the theory that they cling to.

RELIGIOUS BELIEF

While religion continues to flourish in many parts of the world, religious belief is based on history and needs revision, but reluc-tance to change (or to give up control?) is enormous. One example of this occurred in 1939 when the Church of England suppressed their report on spiritualism after the committee had found seven to three in favor of releasing it. Another is the continued refusal by monotheistic religions (Christianity, Islam, and Judaism) to accept reincarnation, despite the overwhelming evidence that now supports it.

In the West, we live in a society that holds conflicting views about life after death. Common attitudes are fear of annihilation and indif-ference. People commonly ask, What use is it to have an answer to the question of what happens to us after death when we cannot influence the situation? Why think of an unpleasant future or no future at all? Fear of pain or of punishment is also common.

Judith Miller's book *Healing the Western Soul* presents statements from two seekers concerning their outlook on death. One ends, "I am concerned by the fear that life is all there is, and after that there is nothing." The other says, "When my six-year-old asked me about death, I just avoided the issue." How sad for those seekers! They were filled with anxiety. How sad for the child, who longed for guidance but got none! Most of us had as little help as that child. We soon realized that asking would not get us beyond the stock religious or physicalist dogmas; we had to accept the vacuum or find our own way as and when opportunities presented themselves.

LACK OF INTEREST

The vital questions surrounding life after death are treated by many of us (curious readers joyfully excepted) with less interest than what to eat for breakfast. What a change from how it was four centuries ago, when religion was the crucial belief, and millions of faith-dissenting Christians died, fighting each other, in the Thirty Years' War. Today, in the West, although religion and physicalist science have opposing dogmas, they are not in open dispute. Both death and discussion of the survival question are taboo, a truly remarkable situation. Do the observers of taboos not care or not dare?

We cannot avoid death, and yet our mainstream society seems to have decided that shutting our eyes to death and after-death awareness is necessary. Socially, this is a seriously destructive situation. With the research evidence that has accumulated in the past 150 years, the support for survival is conclusive, and yet no one talks. Science, with its glorious advances in knowledge and its sparkling technology, makes us comfortable through technology and the sense that we understand many things, while at the same time maintaining a persistent blindness to the beyond. What is beyond death? The answer should help us make sense of our troubled world and empower us to find meaning in our lives. That is what we shall engage with here. This book will show that death is a transition, not the end, and the evidence against physicalist science will grow with every page.

First, a brief interlude. I invite William James, philosopher, medical doctor, and psychologist, who maintains a great reputation more than a century after his death, to tell us about crows. James was no ornithologist, but crows were important to him, as I'll explain.

PROFESSOR WILLIAM JAMES, ORNITHOLOGIST

Professor James was convinced that an unseen world existed and gave much thought to how it could best be demonstrated. Here is his much-quoted statement: "If you wish to upset the law that all crows are black, it is enough if you prove one single crow to be white."

My take on what the professor meant is this: White crows are rare, and so, to skeptical scientists, are anomalous events. We only need to prove the existence of a single white crow (or anomalous event) to disprove the black crow "law." Throughout this book I shall be welcoming these mythological birds from time to time. "Caw!" Did you hear that voice? Don't worry. White crows are friendly birds, and they long to be accepted by curious individuals. Remember Einstein's words? "I have no special talent; I am only passionately curious." We must hope that many more contemporary scientists will shake off the bonds of inappropriate theory and follow Einstein's lead. For now, just remember that we have white crows around us, and give them a friendly welcome.

Now to chapter 1, which introduces individuals and family members as they separate at the time of death and indicates that there is nothing to fear.

CHAPTER 1

Dying in Good Company

Reuniting with Those Who Have Passed

And I will show that whatever happens to anybody, it may be turn'd to beautiful results, and I will show that nothing can happen more beautiful than death. . . .

WALT WHITMAN (1819–1892)

Death is often seen as an event to be postponed for as long as possible. Usually, life comes and goes as a natural day comes and goes. Natural death is a sunset.

Dying and living are essential features of this book. As with night and day, they belong together. Bodily life is a magnificent experience, to be celebrated at the time and afterward. Because this is not everyone's view, and because death is often approached with fear, this opening chapter will focus on the "sunset." We shall look at the end-of-life experience, as recorded by relatives and other caregivers who are with the dying person during those last days and hours. These recordings give us an intimate look at death, as seen by onlookers. In most cases, it is a comforting, joyful experience. It is evident, in many accounts, that those who are dying are not alone. Besides the living caregivers and relatives, they are surrounded by those who have gone ahead and are lovingly awaiting their arrival.

But first, a word about bereavement, a situation with which most of us are only too familiar. Bereavement, too, needs our attention because our feelings at that time depend so much on how we envisage the future. Here is a poem that tells very beautifully the feelings of an individual confronted with the loss of a loved one, although it is not a final loss, simply a change of state.

It is only eight weeks, beloved, since you died.
You left the stiffening inert lump of clay
That was no longer you,
And cried aloud in ecstasy
And suddenly I knew
That all that we believed in,
Lived for, told the world,
Had at its smallest count
Some measure that was true.

It is eight months, beloved, since you died,
And out of my aloneness I have woven strength
To build anew;
For all there was of truth in our relationship
Had eddied, grown, intensified,
Till with a clarion call it sounds
  at the far reaches of the world—
There is no death, no separation of the ways
If man to love prove true.

It is eight years, beloved, since you died,
And for eternity a part of you

Is in its essence me.

I know you are, and in that certainty
Is woven all the fabric of my life.
Gone is all sense of urgency and haste;
For all time now our spirits meet in time.
Loving, we are no longer bound by love;
Heart of my heart, we've set each other free.[1]

We move now to six accounts detailing how death is commonly experienced within the family circle.

Mrs. B. Dies in Childbirth

Mrs. B. died more than a hundred years ago. This account of those who were with her was taken from Death-Bed Visions *by Sir William Barrett, the Dublin physicist who founded the Society for Psychical Research in England and America in the 1880s. His wife was an obstetrician. She gave this account of her patient's last hours.*

When I entered the ward, Mrs B held out her hands to me and said, 'Thank you, thank you for what you have done for me—for bringing the baby. Is it a boy or a girl?' Then, holding my hand tightly, she said, 'Don't leave me, don't go away, will you?' And after a few minutes, while the house surgeon carried out some restorative measures, she lay looking up towards the open part of the room, which was brightly lighted, and said, 'Oh, don't let it get dark—it's getting so dark . . . darker and darker.' Her husband and mother were sent for.

Suddenly she looked eagerly towards one part of the room, a radiant smile illuminating her whole countenance. 'Oh, lovely, lovely,' she said. I asked, 'What is lovely?' 'What I see,' she replied in low, intense tones. 'What do you see?' 'Lovely brightness—wonderful beings.'

It is difficult to describe the sense of reality conveyed by her intense absorption in the vision. Then—seeming to focus her attention more intently on one place for a moment—she exclaimed, almost with a kind of joyous cry, 'Why, it's Father! Oh, he's so glad I'm coming; he is so glad. It would be perfect if only W. (her husband) could come too.'

Her baby was brought for her to see. She looked at it with interest, and then said, 'Do you think I ought to stay for baby's sake?' Then turning towards the vision again, she said, 'I can't—I can't stay; if you could see what I do, you would know I can't stay.' But she turned to her husband, who had come in, and said, 'You won't let baby go to anyone who won't love him, will you?' Then she gently pushed him to one side, saying 'Let me see the lovely brightness.' I left shortly after, and the Matron took my place by the bedside. She lived for another hour and appeared to have retained to the last the double consciousness of the bright forms she saw, and also of those tending her at the bedside, for she arranged with the Matron that her premature baby should remain in hospital till it was strong enough to be cared for in an ordinary household.

FLORENCE E. BARRETT[2]

The hospital matron also wrote an account. This noted that Mrs. B. said her sister Vida was also there to greet her. It was of special interest as Vida's death three weeks earlier had been kept from Mrs. B. because of her illness. The presence of a deceased relative at a deathbed situation used to be considered conclusive evidence that this was indeed a spirit, rather than imagination; however there have been rare cases in which a living person appeared in a deathbed vision.

The coming accounts, from "Jean Cheesman's Dream" to "Final Hours with the Family," are from Peter and Elizabeth Fenwick's book *The Art of Dying*. Each account is given by a relative, and they vary a good deal, but each offers a new look at the process of dying. We start with some accounts in which the dying person became known to others through dreams or on a sudden awakening, at or near the time of death. This is almost invariably a happy greeting, with the assurance that the person is well and glad to be moving on. Interestingly,

3:00 a.m. features as the hour of death in the next three accounts. That's how it was.

Jean Cheesman's Dream

Jean's husband, Vincent, had bipolar disorder. He took his life in February 1989. At the time, Jean and Vincent were separated but remained good friends and very close. She had seen him the previous day, and he had seemed very positive.

She woke up crying at 3 o'clock the next morning, having dreamed that Vincent was sitting on the end of her bed, telling her to stop crying; it was all over, and he was finally at peace.

At eight, she went over to Vincent's flat with the dog, Merlin, and called the police. The coroner's report noted that Vincent had indeed died around 3:00 a.m.

Jean's account demonstrates very well the special quality that these dreams have and that the dreamer recognizes.

Here is yet another account of a relative becoming almost instantly aware of a person's time of death.

Kath's Sudden Awakening

My father was in hospital, and it was in the middle of the night. At the time of his death, around 3 a.m., he visited me and woke me from my sleep. He stood at the end of my bed, just smiling at me and looking down on me. It was the most wonderful and beautiful experience I have ever had; no words were exchanged. I can remember feeling incredibly content and happy, and I drifted back to sleep in a state of euphoria. The next morning, I got up and did my usual chores, forgetting all about the events of the previous night, and then the phone rang. I knew it was my mother, and before she could say anything, I informed her that my father had died last night. She was amazed at my experience.[3]

Angie Feels Her Baby Die

Angie Baird's little girl was born in May 1979. Sadly, the baby was sick with a blood disorder and was kept in the intensive care baby unit. For forty-eight hours she hung on and the doctors were optimistic that the worst was over. Angie writes how she awoke suddenly at 3:00 a.m., shaking and tearful and very anxious about the state of her baby on the floor above. The intensive care unit telephone was engaged, but five minutes later the phone rang to say that the baby had died at precisely 3:00 a.m.

The account shows how sleep is often a time of more intense psychic contact. It also indicates how deep a mother's bond goes, no matter how short the bonding time is.

The following account demonstrates beautifully the peace so commonly gained from the dying process by both the dying and the bereaved. It gives us a glimpse of what each person may experience. The grandmother seemed to be aware, as was Mrs. B., of two realities: the earthly reality peopled by living relatives who are there to give support and the heavenly reality of those who welcome her to the spirit world.

Final Hours with the Family

A ninety-year-old woman is dying of pneumonia at Christmas 2005. As the various members of her family visit her in the hospital, she is able to talk to them very calmly and clearly and is totally "on the ball." As she speaks with her living relatives, it seems that there are many others that she sees around her. Her daughter told that, during the visit of the grandson (the daughter's son), she occasionally said that people were watching over her from the hospital gardens. They would help her "if my head falls forward." She also saw her deceased husband in the hospital room. A little later, "these people" were in the ward, near the windows. She knew her granddaughter couldn't see them—but would understand "when your time comes." She introduced them to her granddaughter as if they were talking to her.

She spoke to her daughter about her future—while referring to "these people," now at the end of her bed. Later she had a three-way conversation with her granddaughter and "these people." She died peacefully only a few hours later.

The Fenwicks comment on how "these people," at first in the garden and finally on the bed, grew closer as death approached. They note that the world in which the woman communicated with her visiting family members became seamlessly interwoven with the other reality, and yet she was fully aware that the two realities were separate. The information she received from "these people" that she would die next morning was correct.

These accounts concerned ordinary people, observed by their relatives, as they left the earth plane on their journey.

Now comes the report of someone who made the crossing and was surprised by the experience. Karl Nowotny, a distinguished Austrian neurologist and psychiatrist, had no belief in survival after death. His sudden death, on April 18, 1965, was a shock to him. In his account of the situation, which his friend Grete received by automatic writing, he recorded that he had felt angry and confused by the experience.

Dr. Nowotny's Surprise

It was a day in spring. I was in my country home, which I only visited occasionally. My health left a lot to be desired. However, I was not bedridden, but went for a walk with friends. It was a lovely evening. As we set off, I was tired and thought I would not be able to walk. But I forced myself and suddenly felt quite healthy and vigorous. I ran forward, breathing in the fresh air deeply, I was as happy as I had not been for a long time. What has happened to me? I wondered that I suddenly had no complaints, no tiredness, no difficulty with breathing? I returned to my friends. But what was this? There

I stood . . . and at the same time I saw myself lying on the ground. The people around were extremely upset and excited. They called a doctor and fetched a car to carry me home. But I was healthy and felt no pain. I could not understand it. I felt the heart of the person lying there. It was not beating. I was dead. But I was alive! I addressed my friends, but they neither saw nor answered me. Then I became angry and went away. But I kept coming back. It was not a pleasant sight, the crying friends who did not want to hear me, and the dead body in front of me, although I felt quite well. And to make matters worse my dog was whimpering desperately. He saw me lying on the ground and he saw me standing next to the body. He did not know which of the two to go to.

After all the formalities had been completed and my body been placed in a coffin, I knew I must have died. But I did not want to believe it. I went to my colleagues at the university. They did not see me or return my greeting. I was very offended. What was I to do? I went up the mountain where Grete lives. She sat there sadly, and also did not hear me. It was no good. I had to face reality. The moment I was aware of the fact I had left the earthly world I saw my good mother. Radiantly she came toward me and told me I was now in the other world. But I could still not believe what I was told. I thought I was dreaming.[4]

Grete, the Vienna-based medium who, after Dr. Nowotny's death, was to receive his messages in automatic writing, had known him well, and they met only three days before his death. The night after their meeting she had a dream in which, to her great surprise, an unknown figure said, "Nowotny is dying." This so impressed her that, two days after his death, she saw a medium who was able to help her transmit an account from Dr. Nowotny by automatic writing. This eventually amounted to six slim volumes titled *Messages from a Doctor in the Fourth Dimension*. Dr. Nowotny's development—to become an active therapist from the afterlife, with a particular interest in spirit release (see chapter 3)—so impressed his friends and associates that they formed the Nowotny Foundation, still a vibrant organization in Austria.

It is good to have evidence from many sources that we can expect dying to be a positive experience. *Deathing,* by Anya Foos-Graber, is one such source. It is an extraordinary book that was written to help us die beautifully. "Deathing," writes Foos-Graber, "has two main aims: to make sure that those who die are comfortable and comforted and to make all of us prepare for the greatest adventure we will face since birth." This will sound crazy to many readers, but hold on; it deserves our full attention. The book grew out of Anya's childhood, when she had many difficulties, including several near-death experiences, which I presume contributed to the skills that she developed to help her spiritual teacher, Paul Twitchell, following his heart attack.

The techniques are based on yoga but go far beyond what is usually taught. The many exercises and techniques, including vibration, breathing, relaxation, sensing, meditation, visualization, chanting, affirmations, the withdrawal of consciousness, and the use of mantras are described in detail in the book. Anya chanted and breathed with Paul to keep his attention focused while he made his transit.

We learn from those who have died that not only is the experience a happy one, but it is usually a transition to a fuller, more beautiful realm of far greater depth and meaning than what we know on Earth. It is a great help to be prepared. The change occurs gradually, and it is often not obvious since the surroundings may appear very similar. People may take time to realize what has happened and may experience confusion and difficulties in adjusting to it. Remember the sunset analogy. After every sunset comes a new dawn.

CHAPTER 2

Near-Death Experience

Sweet Is the Taste!

The most beautiful experience we can have is the mysterious.

ALBERT EINSTEIN (1879–1955)

We are about to enter the enchanted world of the near-death experience. The situation is familiar from the many descriptions. I'll start with a fantasy of the usual experience.

A patient's heart has stopped. It must be started in minutes or she will die. Doctors and nurses are around the bed, fighting a dramatic battle. Unknown to the medics, the patient is experiencing an inner scene just as dramatic as that which involves her body. She hears the doctor say, "She's gone; there's no more we can do." Floating up above the body, she surveys the action below. She looks on with interest but is uninvolved. While watching the medical team at work, she may feel as if her body is no longer hers. She sees aspects of the operating theater that could not be seen from where she lay on the bed.

Now she sees and hears events outside her immediate surroundings, which are later confirmed as correct. She passes along a dark tunnel ending in light that steadily increases in strength and brilliance and yet is not blinding. Surrounded by a heavenly environment, she is met by deceased relatives or religious figures. The peace and love all around are so much better than what earthly life can offer. There may be a life review before a group of "judges," or past events may be flashed before her with great intensity in an instant of time. She longs to stay in this glory of love and light but is told that she still has work to do and must return to her physical body. Death seems far preferable to a return to Earth but to remain here is forbidden. She realizes, perhaps of her own accord or perhaps when she is told by other spiritual presences, that she still has duties to perform in her earthly life. Reluctantly she obeys this demand. However, she will realize later that she has gained from this experience. She no longer fears death and her life has a soaring strength and purpose.

Similar scenes of dying and returning have been described repeatedly.

Cardiologists have been well placed to study these near-death experiences since 1967, when electrical defibrillators resulted in many more survivors of heart attacks. Dr. Pim van Lommel was able to study 344 consecutive cases of cardiac arrest survivors in ten Dutch hospitals; 18 percent of them recounted near-death experiences. One highly promising finding is that following a near-death experience, all fear of dying commonly vanishes. Paradoxically, this can be a mixed blessing, since the change in worldview can lead to social isolation from unbelieving others.

Survivors can expect little support from psychiatrists, who have been very slow to accept that near-death experiences are transcendent experiences. Instead, they are interpreted as responses to physiological, pharmacological, or psychological stressors. Despite official neglect, near-death experience is becoming widely known as a meaningful and highly significant experience, and it is the focus of intensive research worldwide.

Describing one's own death sounds extraordinary to most of us, but to millions of Americans, and to countless others all over the world, through defibrillation, it is the greatest event they can speak of—a truly mind-blowing experience.

Krista Experiences Love as the Answer

Krista was in the hospital to have her baby when her heart stopped for eight minutes. Her breathing ceased and her brain stopped receiving oxygenated blood, but her awareness was unimpaired.

I remember the sound I made as I struggled to get air into my lungs; a tight, frantic gasping. Then, just before everything went dark, a soft, gentle, serenely Divine peace came over me. My heart stopped at 9.18 a.m.

My next moment of awareness was of being high above my body, looking down and seeing it lying there on the bed with people all around me. I could see, and I was still "Krista." I was awake, conscious, yet unencumbered by my physical self. . . .

I had no emotional attachment to the physical forms I saw. The whole scene was almost like watching a movie, and as I watched I became more and more curious about what was happening. I saw my doctor pull my daughter out of my belly and hand her in a blue towel to someone at my right shoulder. They took her quickly and turned around so I couldn't see what they were doing—and I so wanted to see! . . .

As I floated to the other side of the room, I felt myself becoming more and more attached to the scene unfolding below. It felt more familiar, like I almost knew what was going on but couldn't quite grasp it yet. Just as that feeling began to dawn on me, I had the sensation of a tugging from my left side. It was a gentle pull as if to say, "Come on." I resisted, as I wanted to stay and find out what was going on. In response, it pulled harder and I knew intuitively what I was required to do. So, I let go. Once my resistance faded, I found myself shooting to the left like a bullet through the room, through a fluid-like wall, through a flash of bright white space, then out into a place where I was immersed, reabsorbed within the same particulate matter that I was. It was thick and dense and penetrated every bit of me.

What a rush! It was incredible! I zipped along imperceptibly in that space and found myself noticing how the "wall" next to me was fluid in some areas, then densely particulate again. It was beautiful, like a moving piece of art. I felt amazing! Then, in an instant I was permeated with the feeling of sublimely intense, Divinely pure love. It felt as though every single particle that I was, was also that same love. I was absolutely complete and whole and perfect. I was home.

In the next instant I had what I can only describe as a "download" of information—information I'd subconsciously and often consciously wished to have my entire life. I was given the answers to all the questions I'd ever asked. They came to me in a sort of funnel, where instantaneously they all boiled to come down to one point, which was love. It was the same love I felt myself to be at that moment. That very love was the answer to everything! I finally knew![1]

Krista's vivid picture of her extraordinary experience—being out of the body, wishing to stay in the new environment, the dramatic movements on her way home, and the overwhelming sense of love that permeated everything—has much in common with other accounts.

I have recently been reading accounts of children under four years of age who have had near-death experiences. I was struck both by their comments and by their drawings. Here is an account from *What Happens When We Die* by Sam Parnia.

Three-Year-Old John: "When I Died I Saw a Lady"

John's grandmother wrote the following:

John's heart had stopped. . . . There was a lot of commotion . . . they were pressing on his chest and he was lifeless and blue. . . . They put him in an ambulance and took him to hospital . . .

[After he had been discharged from hospital] one day, during the course of play, he said, "Grandma, when I died, I saw a lady." He was not yet three years old. I asked my daughter if anyone had mentioned anything to John about him dying and she said, "No, absolutely not." But over the course of the next few months he continued to talk about his experience. It was all during the course of play and in a child's vocabulary.

He said, "When I was in the doctor's car, the belt came undone and I was looking down from above." He also said, "When you die, it is not the end . . . a lady came to take me. . . . There were also many others who were getting new clothes, but not me, because I wasn't really dead. I was going to come back."[2]

Some children's accounts of near-death experiences only become available years later, when they are adults. The following is one from *The Truth in the Light* by Peter and Elizabeth Fenwick.

The Light Angel Said, "Go Back!"

I started zooming down this really black tunnel at what seemed like 100 mph. Then I saw the enormous, brilliant light at the end, which seemed to take on the shape of an angel. When I reached the light, I heard a voice saying, "Go back, go back," and seeming to will me to make the return journey. I then came back along the tunnel, but very slowly. I couldn't get the experience out of my mind and told my mother. She laughed and thought I'd made the whole thing up. I'll never forget what happened. I can see it all so clearly now all these years later.[3]

Children's near-death experiences are not uncommon. While there was 18 percent incidence of such experiences in the Dutch study of adults who had cardiac arrest, more than 50 percent of children who were close to dying reported similar experiences.[4] In view of the fact that paranormal experiences in general are more common in young children (before their parents have talked it out of them!), this is to be expected.

As often happens when new medical conditions are described,

earlier cases are later identified in hindsight. Albert Heim, a geology professor who taught Einstein, found the same was true with the near-death experiences people had during climbing accidents: they didn't realize until later that what they went through during the accident was actually a near-death experience. The following is Heim's description of his own experience.

Albert Heim's Climbing Accident

Mental activity became enormous, rising to a hundred-fold velocity . . . I saw my whole past life take place in many images, as though on a stage at some distance from me. . . . Everything was transfigured as though by a heavenly light, without anxiety and without pain. The memory of very tragic experiences I had had was clear but not saddening. I felt no conflict or strife; conflict had been transmuted into love. Elevated and harmonious thoughts dominated and united individual images and, like magnificent music, a divine calm swept through my soul. I became ever more surrounded by a splendid blue heaven with delicate and rosy and violet cloudlets. I swept into it painlessly and softly and I saw that now I was falling freely through the air and that under me a snowfield lay waiting.[5]

Heim was knocked unconscious by the fall. The exquisitely peaceful quality of the experience led him to begin collecting other people's observations of climbing accidents. He claimed that, over twenty years of researching the topic, he had discovered that 95 percent of the victims had experienced feelings similar to his own.

A similar event and experience is described in *The Romeo Error*, by Lyall Watson. A nineteen-year-old skydiver who fell from a height of three thousand feet said: "All my past life flashed before my eyes. . . . I saw my mother's face, all the houses I'd lived in, the military academy I'd attended, the faces of friends, everything."[6] He could tell the tale because he had a soft landing and broke only his nose.

Perhaps one of the most famous near-death experiences is Maria's, described in Leslie Kean's *Surviving Death*. Maria's vision of a blue tennis shoe on a hospital roof has become almost legendary.

Maria Spots a Blue Shoe on the Roof

Following a cardiac arrest, Maria felt herself to be floating out of her body toward the ceiling. At first, she watched people working on her body on the ward. Then she found herself outside the hospital. As she rose, she came close to a window on the third floor, the north side, from where she saw "a man's dark blue tennis shoe, well-worn, scuffed on the left side, where the little toe would go. The shoelace was caught under the heel." Later, at Maria's insistence, a staff member, Kimberly Clark Sharp, went to look for the shoe. Nothing could be seen from the outside, so she made the rounds of the rooms on the third floor from the inside. Finally, she came to the right room. Pressing her face against the windowpane and peering down at the ledge, she saw it. From that position she could not see exactly what Maria had seen from outside, the worn spot at the little toe area, but all other details were correct, even the shoelace tucked under the heel. Kimberly opened the window and picked up the shoe. She then saw the scuff mark on the area of the little toe.

While the blue gym shoe is memorable, the essence of these veridical accounts is, in each case, the connection between the reported object or event and the patient's consciousness. Science does not recognize consciousness as such and does not acknowledge that there could be a form that bypasses the brain.

What, then, is the nature of the connection that links the brain and the shoe? That is a challenging mystery, but the mystery contains a nugget of enormous value: brain activity is not invariably essential for consciousness. Because Maria's eyes were closed and her brain nonfunctional, normal vision was impossible. What happened was beyond our present concepts of normality. The patient was in no doubt about the location of the shoe and was able to describe its appearance in minute detail. This could not be dismissed as a dream. The experience was so compelling that it demanded confirmation. Once confirmed, it became history.

What does this mean for us? What does it mean for the philosophy of science and how we see the world? The experience shows that in certain situations the brain is unnecessary; we can do without it and gain information, which is later confirmed. That is an undeniable, thought-stretching truth.

Philosopher, psychiatrist, and physician Raymond Moody came to identify the near-death experience as a condition in the late 1960s. How did he come to be the trailblazer who drew attention to an extraordinary anomaly that was not uncommon and yet had been largely concealed by the percipients for fear of derision? First, he heard a psychiatrist, George G. Ritchie, author of *Return from Tomorrow,* tell privately how he had died and then came back. Then he heard a woman tell how her grandmother had a similar experience. The two remarkable stories were so similar that Moody began to look for others. His work as philosophy lecturer gave him the opportunity to discuss mortality with his students. He did this, without telling them of these two accounts, and found that listeners often had similar stories of their own.

Moody began to give talks on the subject and had many other cases brought to his attention. After several years he had more than a hundred cases for his book, *Life after Life.* He provided a societal awareness of the near-death experience and its extraordinary nature and effects. His identification of near-death experience caught the imagination of his first readers, and now it is known the world over.

Death approaches, but contrary to nearly all religious views, with it come love and light and beauty. From now on, nearly every chapter in this book, directly or indirectly, will be a confirmation of that promise. Oh! Listen to that. Did you hear it? It was a little faint at first, but then it came loud and clear and very confident. Yes, of course you heard. "Caw! Caw! Cawww!" Beautiful, wasn't it?

CHAPTER 3

Spirit Release

Time to Move On

Taking a new step, uttering a new word, is what people fear most.

F. M. DOSTOEVSKY (1821–1881)

When, at fifty-nine, I finally returned, after twenty years, to clinical psychiatry, I had no idea that I was on the verge of an inconceivably strange adventure. Treating patients by talking to troublesome earthbound spirits could not have been further from my thoughts. And yet, three years later, I was doing just that. My decision to write a book on survival after physical death came out of my work with earthbound spirits and their connection to the dying process.

To clarify the situation, I'll give a brief explanation of what, to my knowledge, happens at death, when the soul passes for further development to the Light, the entrance to the spirit world. It fits what souls report to therapists during spirit release. Mediums may receive similar information. This transition is not invariable. If the soul has no concept of survival or if death is traumatic and unexpected, the Light may not be visible, and attachment may occur to someone at the scene. Sometimes attachment occurs by design. Addiction to alcohol, drugs, some other worldly activity, or an intense relationship with another person can result in a soul remaining earthbound by intention. This may become a parasitic connection that is difficult to break. A soul may also be stranded in some familiar location and produce effects, such as haunting, or it may attach to another living individual, either knowingly or unknowingly. Such a spirit may move on of its own accord, but there may be a need for release.

The practice of spirit release—or exorcism, as it is called when part of a religious practice—goes back thousands of years and continues to be used by religions worldwide. In Brazil, Spiritism, founded by Allan Kardec, born Hyppolite Rivail, has many hospitals and thousands of treatment centers, where spirit release by mediums is a main feature of the treatment. There are many other regions, especially in India and Africa, where it is an important part of the social fabric for practitioners of spirit release using local techniques to remove harmful spirits induced as curses (spirit interference).

My personal knowledge and experience concern spirit attachment in the industrialized Western world, where the condition, although prevalent, is rarely acknowledged. Except for its use by mediums who need spirit guides for their work, attachment is usually an unwished-for condition in which spirits interfere with the healthy functioning of individuals. I have been concerned mostly with the earthbound souls of those who have died. Some nonhuman spirits (entities) or demonic spirits can also cause problems.

How does one make a diagnosis of spirit attachment in such cases? Since most patients are ignorant of the condition, the most important step is for them to become aware that such a condition may be present. Any of the following symptoms may manifest: low energy level, character shifts or mood swings, impulsive behavior, memory gaps, poor concentration, sudden onset of anxiety or depression, abuse of alcohol or drugs, hearing a negative inner voice. It is very rare for attached spirits to take full control, but such cases have been described. Nearly always, the intrusion shows only moderate effects, as in my patient Pete, whom you will shortly be meeting.

The concept of spirit interference raises many questions, such as, How do spirits gain entry, and how can we protect ourselves against these secret intruders? While there is no doubt that some people are far more open to spirit interference than others, those who lead healthy lives, without extremes of abuse or indulgence, are the least likely to be troubled.

Attached spirits should be encouraged to go to the Light. Even if not harmful, they may be doorways for harmful spirits to enter. Dealing with them requires special skill. To assist the transition, I ask for the help of a deceased relative of the patient or, if none is apparent, a spirit guide. Such help is often perceived by the patient and leads to effective release. Remote spirit release may be used by therapists with psychic abilities. They scan clients for attached spirits and clear them with or without the aid of spirit guides.

Talking to inner voices is not part of regular psychiatric practice, and I need scarcely say that it did not feature in my formal training. It was only after my meeting with Lance Trendall, the hypnotist whom I mentioned in the introduction, and subsequent training in hypnosis and spirit release, that this door opened for me. I used it first with my nonpsychotic patients at Fairfield Hospital, especially those who had treatment-resistant depressive and anxiety states. Most of them were keen to use hypnosis and glad of an opportunity to change from the usual medication. Without mentioning the possibility of attached spirits, I would have them, while in hypnosis, look into an imaginary mirror or imagine being filled with light and look for shadowy areas. I would then ask, "If that area could make a noise (or speak), what might it say?" A response would usually lead to a verbal exchange, with the possibility of exploring the history of an attached spirit. However, in the absence of a verbal response, it was often possible to communicate by finger signals. I would ask the spirit if it could relate its own experience of physical death, and why it had joined the patient. Attached spirits usually have their own problems that need to be resolved. Sometimes a spirit has a past-life connection to the patient that needs to be explored before a release can occur.

Physical Symptoms Resulting from Spirit Attachment

Innumerable hospital investigations had failed to reveal the cause of Pete's trouble. He worked as a senior manager and professional trainer and had a very successful career. Pete came to me as a last resort, after being offered a marvelous job opportunity abroad. It was a chance that, at fifty, he couldn't afford to lose. Before he came, emails from both husband and wife had delivered a daunting catalog of complaints: abdominal pain, joint pains, retching and diarrhea, wide fluctuations in temperature, and periods of severe prostration. Life had become a misery. Had it not been for a wonderfully sustaining and rich marital relationship, he might not have survived.

There were two important clues to the cause of the problem. One had come to light a year before, when, during hypnotic regression, Pete had experienced a life in Tibet. As a boy, while being schooled to be a lama, he had been bayoneted to death by a Chinese soldier. The other clue was his conviction of being possessed. How this came about he could not say. He had first felt it after the death of his mother years before. In Pete's words, "This thing lives in my descending colon. This is its lair. I can show you the exact place. It can be small or large. When it's really at rest it's about the size of a big marble. When it's fully active it penetrates and permeates my entire body, including my brain. At its worst I feel that it's killing me by draining all my energy and by consuming my cells and preventing my mind from functioning. It is almost never absent." I had Pete relax through visualization and imagine his body filled with light. He described "a dark, triangular kind of shape" on the left side of the abdomen. What follows in the next account is the verbatim dialogue between me, Pete, and the entity speaking through Pete.

Alan: *If it could make a noise, what noise would it make?*

Pete: *Constant, intense. A raging scream.*

Alan: And if that scream could find words, what words would come?

Pete: Hatred.

> [A nonhuman entity then identifies itself as Askinra;
> in appearance, it's "like a dark flame."]

Askinra (speaking through Pete): I shouldn't be in here. I feel trapped like this.

> [Askinra becomes aware of voices and light.]

Angels: Come back! Come out!

> [Askinra feels blocked.]

Askinra: I can only come through him.

Alan: Tell me, Askinra, what effect are you having on Pete?

Askinra: I'm destroying him. If I destroy him, then I can be free.

Alan: Become aware of the angels that are calling your name, and tell me what you see.

Askinra: It is as if a pathway goes up through the heart to the top of the head.

Alan: And where does it lead beyond the head?

Askinra: Into another place that's very different from this one. It is outside this reality. It's the place I'm trying to go, but I can't get there, I can't get through. Every time I try to get out, I can't get through.

Alan: At what point are you stopped, Askinra? Try and get through and tell me what your experience is.

Askinra: It's like a closed door . . . like something that's locked.

Alan: Describe the closed door.

Askinra: It's round and white, like bone.

Alan: Askinra, speak to the closed door that's round and white, like bone. Ask the closed door, "May I come through?" How does it respond?

Askinra: No.

Alan: Ask the closed door, "What must I do so that you will open for me?"

Askinra: Die!

Alan: Askinra, are you telling me that you are able to die? You are an immortal spirit, Askinra, how can you die?

Askinra: That's what the door is for; it's for the time of death.

> [This path of inquiry seems to be blocked. I decide on another approach.]

Alan: Askinra, tell me, how old was Pete when you joined him?

Askinra: Twelve.

> [Askinra entered at the time of the fatal bayonet wound, during the Chinese invasion of Tibet when Pete was twelve in that incarnation, preparing to become a lama. It seems that Askinra was there and was taken by surprise.]

Askinra: Hatred pushes me in there and fixes me in there.

> [Pete gives permission for me to speak to the soldier.]

Alan: I'm speaking to the soldier who is putting the bayonet into this boy of twelve, who feels so much hatred. You, the soldier, what do you have to say? You can speak to me. You're feeling anger, aren't you? What do you say to the little boy?

Soldier: You have to be destroyed!

Alan: And you hate this boy.

Soldier: I hate everything he stands for.

> [The soldier, who on questioning reveals that his name is Chen Ling, now regrets his action. With angelic help, Chen Ling removes his anger from the bayonet thrust. As an indication of his regret, Chen Ling gives the boy a tiny pearl. Askinra is now able to pass through the door in the head, which opens onto a place of mountains and light. Spirit guides are requested. The hand of the guide feels "like a cool stream."]

Askinra: Sorry, I never meant to be there. Come and find me in the new place.

Afterward, Pete experienced some parting spasms in the left

abdomen, but he felt much lighter. Healing spirits were called in to cleanse and heal the whole subtle energy system, leaving Pete feeling good. A month later, Pete described the experience: "The physical symptoms have gone. It was just as distinct as if you were carrying something and it weighed a certain amount and it had a certain texture and a certain feeling to it and that thing was removed from you. With that thing out of the way, I'm free to think and feel and to be aware in ways that I wasn't before. It has made a huge difference."

At a ten-year follow-up Pete wrote the following:

The immediate result of Alan's work with me was that I was instantly relieved of a wide range of intensely debilitating physical symptoms upon which all other approaches, both "allopathic" and "alternative," had been ineffective. My mental and emotional stance also changed for the better. I had more clarity and felt more con-tented and happy with my present circumstances and substantially more positive about the future. It is not the case that everything in my life was perfect after this event, or that I never suffered again from either physical illness or emotional upset, but it is for me a fact that this was one of the major turning points in my life and that, in many ways, I never looked back. My experience was, essentially, that of being freed from "something" that had trapped me in a lim-ited and painful version of my Self. Since then, my life and work have been successful in a number of ways that I did not, previously, anticipate.

The case of Askinra is a white crow, waiting to be acknowledged. And it was a beautiful crow, wasn't it? I loved the gift of the small pearl and the hand of the guide feeling "like a cool stream," and Askinra's invitation to Pete to come and find him in the new place. "Caw!"

What else can be said about the preceding account? Even twenty such cases with successful outcomes would not be sufficient to change current concepts. Much repetition by others would be required. Even if the clinical success of spirit release were to be confirmed, it would be held to contravene basic principles of scientific belief and practice. For this reason, many would consider it impossible to include spirit release therapy in the body of accepted psychiatric concepts and procedures.

Spirit attachment, along with near-death experiences and many other phenomena supporting the spiritual worldview, has yet to be accepted as evidence of consciousness unrestricted by the brain. But what we must remember here is that what is theoretically impossible may be undeniable truth. There may be theoretical "impossibilities" that observations insist upon but that physicalist science cannot prove. The physicalist view is largely based on assumptions, such as the view that human consciousness is created by brain activity. And yet we don't believe that the TV program is created by the TV set.

When will psychiatry be able to take spirit attachment and spirit release therapy off the "impossibilities" list? It will happen, of that I have no doubt. In chapter 11, "Hypnotic Regression," we shall find other "impossibilities" that have been confirmed many times over but are still not accepted by physicalist science. Observation will continue to question theory. Acceptance is a matter of time.

Spirit attachment can also have sexual features that usually inhibit the affected individual from seeking help. Here is a patient of mine (I'll call her Denise) who found her own method of protection from sexual harassment by the incubus at an earlier age.

Incubus Removed

Already as a young girl, I was aware that something not OK was happening to me. During the night I could feel an energy that touched me in different places on my body. They were very sexual touches. I didn't dare to say a word to my parents for fear of being called a liar. This kind of situation happened on and off.

Growing up and reading different books about paranormal

phenomena, I realised that these were entities which certainly were sex addicts while alive and still needed to satisfy their lust even though they had no body anymore. To get rid of these bad forces when they were attacking me, I realised that just calling Archangel Michael and even just thinking about the archangel made them stop. One day I explained my problem to a good friend who is very versed in Indian culture and in drawing yantras (mystical diagrams with high vibrations). She drew one for me to hang over my bed. From that moment on these negative forces didn't bother me anymore. What a relief! I can't help asking the question, Why did I, and no doubt other women, have to experience this trouble?

Denise's account highlights an experience that may be common but is unrecognized. Even though we do not know the cause of a condition, or how to help with conventional approaches, it may sometimes be appropriate to follow the practices of other cultures. Do doctors ask about it? I didn't. I expect that goes for the great majority.

We now go to Edwin for another account of spirit release. It also has a past-life connection, and although it is very different from the connection in the previous accounts, it is again an unwelcome one. But also like the case just described, it too has a happy ending. Spirit attachment is a common condition, but it varies considerably in severity. Hypnosis makes it easy to diagnose and to treat in most cases. Pete was effectively treated in one session of hypnotherapy. Though I am no longer in touch with Pete, he was well eight years later and continuing his very successful work.

Spirit Release: An Ancient Jealousy

Jealousy is a failure of love. It is agonizing to admit and devastating to our life's course and purpose. Edwin, an esteemed life coach, was a fifty-year-old "agony aunt" (advice columnist) who was himself in agony as he consulted me. The relationship with his male partner was in trouble. His jealousy, a lifelong problem, had become unbearable. Jealousy and suspicion, he told me, had featured even at school. There had been several male partners and one female (the longest and the most painful relationship) early on. Wreckage strewed the way behind him, and it was getting worse.

"In recent weeks," he said, "jealousy and suspicion have been almost unbearable, almost to the point where I was thinking that maybe I needed medication or something like that. I was worried that I was getting depressed as well, as it took up so much of my mind space."

Only recently he had spoken to a friend and found himself saying, "It's almost like I am somebody else." As soon as he said that, he continued, "there was a big 'aha!' moment and immediately I felt separate from the feelings. It was as if, for the first time, I could sense what was mine and what belonged elsewhere. The relief and weight that I felt lift was tremendous. I knew then that I could control the feelings." How many people would have done that? Awareness of spirit attachment is virtually unknown to both patients and psychiatrists.

Of the jealousy, Edwin said, "It's like someone talking to me who gives me pictures. I'm totally overwhelmed by thoughts and images, so that I can think of nothing else. At times I feel that I might as well finish it off—no point in carrying on. It's like a thunderstorm, a brain storm. It's the worst kind of jealousy, possessiveness, control, paranoia. It seems like there's this very vengeful female entity around. It feels like I'm being held hostage by a woman." That was the essence.

Spiritual issues are often best explored in altered states of consciousness, so at our second session I used hypnosis. Edwin was soon in a trance. My first aim was to contact Edwin's higher self, that part of the soul that often knows much more than is available to the conscious mind.

We'll pause a moment while I explain a difference between my work with Pete and that with Edwin, twelve years later. I knew nothing about the involvement of the higher self when I worked with Pete. That knowledge came later, from Tom Zinser's book, Soul-Centered Healing, *which taught that the higher self is a part of the soul and essential in treatment, as a sort of cotherapist. After that, I consulted the higher self at the start of treatment in every patient where I suspected that an entity (a spirit or an ego state) might be present.*

After setting up finger signals (one finger for "yes," another finger for "no"), I asked Edwin's higher self if there were any spirit entities present. I learned that there were seven. The first entity to come forward was Mary, a domestic servant who said she had died violently in England in 1879. In my dialogue with Mary, I have omitted some parts, retaining only essential details. Speaking through Edwin's voice, Mary said that a female entity, later identified as Helena, was already present.

> *[Helena whispers to Edwin, telling him all kinds of things; she makes him afraid.]*

Alan (speaking to Helena): *How old was Edwin when you came?*

Helena: *I was with him before that.*

Alan: *You were with him before he was born?*

Helena: *Oh yes. I followed him through time.*

Alan: *Were you together in some way?*

Helena: *I left my husband for him.*

Alan: *Did you spend the rest of your life with Edwin?*

> *[At that, Helena laughs dismissively. They were together for just two or three days.]*

Helena: *That was it. He had his way and he left. I sat in that room, waiting, waiting, waiting.*

> *[He never came. Helena shot herself.]*

Helena: *In those last minutes, I vowed that I would make him suffer the way that he made me suffer.*

Alan: *Be aware of what happens when your body dies, and you leave it. What happens next?*

Helena: My first thing is, I'm going to find him. Looking back on it I can't believe . . . It makes me angry. I wasted my life. I'd kind of given up on my life. I'm going to make him suffer. The pain is still there, every day, every moment. Now when he's waiting for someone, I come in: "What are they doing? Are they doing this? Are they doing that?"

Alan: Edwin, have you got thoughts about what you would like to do in order to resolve the situation? My own feeling is that I should ask Helena if she would be happy to receive Light from the higher self.

[Edwin agrees.]

Alan: Higher self, is there anything I need to know about Helena before I ask her if she's willing to receive Light from you?

Higher self: She needs to know the rest of the story. She thinks that Edwin abandoned her. It was an accident, falling off a horse.

Alan: Helena, have you been hearing that conversation? It seems to shed rather a different light on things.

Helena: I've been an awful fool!

Alan: What do you think about that?

Helena: All this time . . . I believed . . . he didn't come back for a reason. I thought it was all about me. I never knew. This is like . . . I never, never . . . Oh my God! I'm in shock!

Alan: May I suggest some very important first aid? I suggest that the higher self sends you some Light. May I do that?

[Helena agrees.]

Alan: Higher self, please send Light to Helena. Let me know when you've done that. Helena, are you receiving Light? How's that feeling? Does it feel good?

Helena: In my head is peace. And there's this understanding. It wasn't to do with me.

Alan: It must be a wonderful relief to you. I'm going to speak to Edwin now. Edwin, how does that feel? It must have made a difference.

Edwin: Yes, a lot of difference!

Alan: We must explore a little bit about how things are with the others, how Helena comes to terms with that revelation, and what she wants to do about it. And I presume that you would be happy for Helena and for everyone to move on.

[Edwin agrees.]

Helena, you're feeling better now, aren't you?

Helena: Much.

Alan: Before you go, I would just ask you about the situation here with Edwin and the others.

Helena: They seem to have dispersed. . . . It seems that now that my story is complete, the energy that was holding them here has gone.

[Helena goes to the Light.]

Alan: Higher self, are there other things that need to be done?

Helena: Edwin needs to write the story, so they can be complete.

[I put the following questions to Edwin two years later.]

Alan: Describe your feelings during the session.

Edwin: During the session, you talked directly to Helena, I was aware of what was happening, but it was as if I was sitting to one side calmly listening to what was being said. When Helena revealed the story, I was totally surprised, as this was not in my thinking at all. As more of the story became clear, it all suddenly made sense. Instead of feeling angry and irritated with Helena's interference, I felt compassion and understanding for her. No negotiation was necessary as she was happy to move on. For both of us a weight had been lifted from our negative chatter and importantly from our hearts.

Alan: What were the effects of the session during the following days and weeks?

Edwin: The effects were immediate. In the days that followed I understood any internal chatter was my own relating to my own life experiences, it really was that clear and distinguishable. I continue to feel free. In my session, I promised Helena that I would honor her by sharing our story, and that promise has been kept by sharing our story as part of your book, and so our story is complete.

Alan: Have these effects lasted?

Edwin: Yes.

Alan: What effect has this had on your present life?

Edwin: The sessions not only had an internal effect, but the work also changed the way I relate in personal relationships. A few months after my work with you, my then relationship ended as I felt worthy enough and no longer guilty. I was able to challenge unacceptable behavior. I felt liberated and free. I had a brief relationship afterward that didn't last, but my behavior and the dynamics were very different, and the real test was that there was no doubting, suspicious, internal voice. That in itself made the relationship a valuable experience. I am eternally grateful to you for your support and expertise in helping me regain my own life, and for bringing peace to Helena.

Edwin's recovery was a joint effort. He knew of my work and of the troubles that spiritual interference can cause. The higher self, the part of the soul that is incarnate and keeps an eye on things, but can help only if asked, was aware of the dynamics. My question about sending Light opened the door. Realizing that her anger came from a misunderstanding, Helena was happy to leave. A serious, intractable problem was readily resolved. Without Edwin's awareness of my work, this could not have happened. A white crow flew to heaven. Edwin was relieved, and so was I.

CHAPTER 4

Gender Dysphoria Resolved by Spirit Release

*Please call me by my true names, So I can hear all my
    cries and my laughs at once,
So I can see that my joy and my pain are one.
Please call me by my true names, so that I can wake up,
And so the door of my heart can be left open.*

Тнісн Nнaт Hanн (1926–2022)

In chapter 3 we learned how the release of an attached female spirit had cured Edwin's depression and anxiety in just one session. Now, we shall learn how Dr. Fiore's patient, Roger, with the diagnosis of gender dysphoria, responded to a similar treatment. It is important to note that dysphoria means discomfort or dissatisfaction with the gender a person feels anatomically. It does not imply gender abnormality. I've found very little on the spiritual treatment of gender dysphoria in psychiatric literature. There is much more in the spiritual treatment path to be explored. Although gender dysphoria is increasingly presented for consultation, the cause remains unknown. The usual surgical reassignment aims simply for symptom relief. Meanwhile, it seems wise to keep an open mind on the matter.

The account comes from *Opening the Closed Door,* a book by Edith Fiore, who generously allowed me to include her case here. Despite having to condense it somewhat, I hopefully have retained its substance. Dr. Fiore, who kindly wrote the foreword to my book, is an American psychologist, famed for her unconventional and highly skilled professional work.

Spirit Release: Gender Dysphoria

Roger is an internationally recognized physician, who has presented more than sixty papers throughout the world on his work. His specialty is on the cutting edge of modern medicine. Besides being a scientist, he is a caring healer whose life's work eases the pain of the dying.

[Roger said,] "I've been diagnosed as having a severe gender dysphoria by the psychiatrists at the Center and [the diagnosis was] corroborated with a whole battery of psychological tests."

I asked him why he agreed to see me.

He frowned and said, "[My wife] gave me an ultimatum. Mary read your book, *The Unquiet Dead,* two weeks ago, and forced me to read it. She feels that I'm possessed by a female spirit." He smiled contemptuously, but quickly continued, "And a friend of Mary's, a very sensitive person, claims to have actually seen this woman. I've also been depressed for the past six months. Actually, I was suicidal because of the terrific conflict I feel. The psychiatrist I've been seeing put me on Prozac. At first it affected me negatively. I'd be very tired and hyper in the morning, and I'd have ups and downs. Now it's fine. And drinking and anger are other issues I've been dealing with, not too successfully. When I joined the gender program four months ago, I cut out all hard alcohol. But in the last week, I've been abusing beer and wine." . . .

At this point, I decided to give Roger some feedback. I told him that I felt quite strongly that he did have a female spirit with him. I said, "She isn't satisfied with your male body and wants a female one. She may not even realize that her own body has died and that she is possessing you. A great number of possessing spirits are in denial; they just don't want to accept their deaths. It may be that she joined you during your ski vacation, especially since you may have weakened your aura's protection by drinking after a day of skiing."

He blurted out, "I'm not at all sure I can accept this spirit possession hypothesis. I've always felt, and my therapists agree, that it's what happened in my early childhood. I believe that my gender identity issue got set by my mother."

I added, "Roger, that is how most therapists would see it. It makes sense. But remember, you had years of no conflict, and then nine years ago, it surfaced abruptly and strongly. That's why I think possession is the cause of the problem. Let's use our remaining time today, which is just about 30 minutes, and I'll do a generalized depossession and then a mini depossession specifically for a female. Then tomorrow, we may do a regression to your childhood and explore that as a cause. Hopefully, at least we can release some entities today, whether or not they are in any way causing or contributing to the problem. As a physician, you've spent a lot of time during your training and since then in hospitals. I've found that doctors, nurses, aides, and ambulance drivers usually have picked up a great number of spirits."

Roger agreed to the depossessions. After reclining in the chair, I covered him with a lavender mohair blanket. He closed his eyes, and I began the hypnotic induction.

As I did the first, generalized depossession, I noticed obvious signs of anxiety. His breathing became shallow and rapid. The pulses on the sides of his neck speeded up. When I told the spirits that their loved ones were present to help them, tears rolled down his cheeks. Finally, at the end, his whole body relaxed, and his face seemed content.

After bringing him out of hypnosis, I asked what he had experienced. He proved to be quite clairvoyant, which about 50 percent of my patients appear to be under hypnosis. He saw many spirits leave with their loved ones.

I asked him to close his eyes again and then did the depossession for the female spirit, whom I assumed was present. His face and body first registered fear and then became calmer as I spoke of the beautiful and youthful body she would have when she went into the spirit world with her loved ones. When I mentioned the exquisite wardrobe that she could have, a big smile broke out on Roger's face. This time it was not a smile of contempt, but one of happiness. I ended the depossession and brought him out of hypnosis.

He announced, "Her name is Natalie. She couldn't wait to leave! She knew I'd make a lousy woman, being as tall as I am. When she heard that she could have her own perfect female body, she was overjoyed. That's what she really wanted, and had settled for second best. When you mentioned her wardrobe, that did it!"

I asked him what he thought of it now.

He frowned, "It was too real to doubt. But, it's too easy. How could just a few minutes resolve such an enormous problem?"

I said, "It does sometimes. Let's hope that's the case with you. The proof of the pudding is in the eating, so time will tell. Observe yourself carefully and let me know tomorrow if there are any changes."

We ended the first of two double, 100-minutes, sessions. I felt we had developed a rapport and that Roger was now cooperating fully in his treatment. . . .

The next morning, my first appointment was with Roger. I eagerly walked out to the waiting room and immediately noticed that he was a changed man. He smiled broadly and bounded up from his chair. As soon as he stepped into my consulting room, he announced, "She's gone!"

Sitting down, he leaned forward and stated animatedly, "I feel different. But, 1 must admit I feel melancholy, like I've lost a friend. I know now I can control my own destiny, certainly more than before. Anyway, she needs a male lover. She came back later to show me how she looked. She has long blond hair, much better than my wig. And, a perfect figure. Her face is beautiful! I feel so happy for her." . . .

"Somehow, I've become more spiritual, if you can understand that."

I replied, "You probably released a lot of spirits, who were keeping you from being yourself. You'll be finding a lot of things changing. Even if you were just free of her influence, it would be as though an enormous burden has been lifted from you."

He proudly said, "I had less of an inclination to drink. I had a few beers, but didn't overdo it."

I told him that I'd like to check out using a hotline to his subconscious mind to see if there are any spirits still here. I said, "I'll establish finger signals, and your inner mind will answer my questions directly. Your subconscious will lift and lower your fingers without any help or interference from your conscious mind. Your subconscious mind knows exactly what is going on within you. It knows how many spirits you've had, how many have left, and not only that, but how many are still here. Finger signals can be very helpful. We'll release as many as possible. After that, I'll do some regressions to cover all bases."

Under hypnosis, Roger had no trouble establishing finger signals, a yes and no finger, that his inner mind used to answer my questions. Through them, we learned that the person responsible for his gender dysphoria had left. He still had four additional spirits with him, three males and one female. They all left readily with their loved ones.

Since we had time remaining in our session, I asked his inner mind if one of his past lives was having a strong negative impact on him in terms of the gender dysphoria. His "yes" finger flipped up.

He regressed quickly and easily and saw himself as a little girl in a pretty dress playing outside and having a good time. When I asked him to move to a later time, he seemed puzzled and then stated, "She's having trouble getting older. I didn't get older." I asked his inner mind to take him to one hour before her death. He mumbled, "She's in bed. She looks awful. Her mother is concerned. She's not."

He whispered, "Now she's gone." When I asked him how she felt once she was out of her body, he answered, "She feels good. She's warm. She's going toward a bright light, and she feels happy."

As we continued our work, he went to the lifetime that was responsible for his karma, the possession that resulted in his gender identity issue. After a death as a young woman, the spirit wanted a man and went to him. She chose him because he was big and strong, and she felt he could protect her. The man was weakened by her presence, confused, and couldn't understand what had happened to him, why he had changed so drastically. He felt feminine. She stayed with him for ten years and left when he aged and was no longer strong. She realized she had made a mistake. She went into the spirit world where she met someone whom she loved. He told her he was displeased with her, that her behavior was wrong. She was very remorseful and cried. Her mentor told her she would have to pay for her actions. She would have to have years of unhappiness, but that she would eventually be freed.

Roger confided, "That woman came back as me. My mother is looking at her belly, wishing, praying for a girl. She almost got her wish!"

I stated that the little girl, who died, was not he in his last incarnation, but the possessing spirit was who he was during his immediate past life.

Four days after our session, Roger wrote me a letter in which he expressed his gratefulness for my help. He added, "I saw Natalie briefly Sunday. She is very happy and grateful to all of us. I asked to see her lover. They were slightly impatient young lovers, so I didn't keep them long." . . .

Just as I finished writing up the chapter on Roger, I got an inspiration to call him to see how he is. It's been a year since we've talked on the phone or had any communication.

Roger was more than delighted to hear from me. Thirty minutes before I called him, he had just finished a letter to me, which was to be mailed the next day. He said "It can't be a coincidence!" He reported that he was doing fine. Then he announced, "The gender dysphoria is a thing of the past!"[1]

So that was it! Roger was considering suicide to alleviate his gender dysphoria, but Dr. Fiore was able to release the spirit that was tormenting him.

Advising those with gender identity questions is really difficult, as the decision to change one's gender is such an individual matter. After her retirement Dr. Fiore referred to me two cases who had contacted her from England. I was excited to see them. Neither of them had reached the near-operation stage. One was a young man who already had the sense of having a young woman with him and decided to continue with a male body and leave things as they were. The other was a young woman whose parents were opposed to a change on which she was determined. Whether or not she had a male spirit with her was unclear, since she was in no mood to explore the situation.

I once attended a conference on gender dysphoria. At the break I spoke to the specialist who was chairing the conference and told him of a case from a specialist medical journal describing a patient who had decided on a nonmedical approach and had seen an exorcist, with satisfying results. He had returned to being fully male. The conference chair knew it well, having been editor of the journal in which it was reported. He was not convinced. Two years, he said, was too short a follow-up period.

Beliefs depend very much on the believer. The important thing, of course, is how the patient feels.

CHAPTER 5

A Spirit Guide Advises

Dr. Thomas Zinser

Dr. Thomas "Tom" Zinser, the psychotherapist who taught me that the higher self is a part of the soul and essential in therapy, has brought tremendous advances to the treatment and knowledge of the human subconscious mind. Tom has written three books that describe his approach and therapeutic process: *Soul-Centered Healing: A Psychologist's Extraordinary Journey into the Realms of Sub-Personalities, Spirits, and Past Lives* and *The Practice of Soul-Centered Healing,* volumes one and two. This chapter details his connection with a spirit guide on the Other Side with whom he worked for twenty-five years.

Tom Meets Gerod, a Spirit Guide

Katherine Mackey was a secretary at the hypnotherapy practice where Tom worked. She was blessed with a spirit guide called Gerod. One day Katherine heard Tom discussing psychic experience with another therapist. She suggested to Tom that she arrange a session with her guide, using automatic writing. That Saturday, August 1, 1987, Tom sat at a table next to Katherine, who duly went into a trance and began to write.

"Gerod is here with you now, Katherine. Is Tom there also?"

And he was.

"Good, I will be happy to talk with him as you asked me to do."

Tom asked for advice about Jim, a patient with whom therapy was stuck. He gave Gerod no other information. Katherine's hand began to write:

"Jim is possessed by a low-level spirit trying to adhere to earth. You can instruct Jim on ways to strengthen his soul and tell Jim he must ask this spirit to leave him. He is a good person growing well but he is not fully aware of his potential life with spirit guides, hence his confusion. A person more aware would have recognized the low-level state of this guide."[1]

This information about spirits obsessing his clients was news to Tom. He had read about spirits but had not worked with them, since it was not a part of his professional training. At his next session with Jim, using hypnosis, Tom addressed this presumed spirit and managed to persuade him to leave Jim. It worked! This was a great help to Jim, who was soon able to manage his life without therapy.

That meeting completely changed Tom's view on what psychotherapy could achieve. It opened up a whole new world that neither he nor his colleagues had previously taken into account. With Gerod's help, Tom got to know his clients at a much deeper level. Not only did he learn about the life of spirits, he also learned about ego states, which are parts of a personality created internally by the soul as a protective response to emotional trauma. Remarkably, ego states have the ability to respond to therapy like separate individuals with their own thoughts and perceptions.

Using hypnosis, Tom set up a therapeutic system of communicating by which an ego state could move the patient's fingers, while the patient was hypnotized, to indicate "yes," "no," or "don't know" in response to Tom's questions. Working with ego states became a great way to promote positive change in people who came to Tom for emotional help. As Tom and Gerod became familiar with each other, Katherine, in her trance state, learned to let Gerod communicate not just through automatic writing but also by using her voice, so that communication with Tom became more fluent. This was quite a break, and one that later gave rise to Tom's books.

Here is more from Gerod from that first meeting. The writing tells of souls freed from bodies. They are called discarnates.

Discarnate personalities are usually inhabitants of the spirit levels. Your work with your patients has opened up an area I believe has not been too well explored, as you may know. People with souls attract to themselves discarnates. Gerod is a discarnate, but there are many of us, and many of us are not able to successfully function as guides. Unfortunately, these spirits become excess baggage for some earth-existing people.

This is how Gerod described the situation that first day:

Gerod is a teacher of persons to stimulate growth of the soul in order that a person may grow toward the Light and so closer to God, as Katherine calls the Light. 'I am a high-level guide interested in growth through the attainment of loving attitudes on earth. I have lived in a level of spiritual existence only. I have not been an earth-dweller but have great interest and love for the loving natures of earth-experience persons and so have elected to be a teaching guide to you there. I am not good at fortune telling, table tapping or the Michigan lottery.'

Spirit guides are sometimes known as guardian angels. It seems we all have guides. In some circles, it is common to make fun of such ideas. This is because science has such control over our thinking. Science (including psychiatry) treats spirit guides as delusions.

Tom learned a vast amount from Gerod. In his treatment sessions, he received much guidance from questioning the higher self of the patient, which in Katherine Mackey's book *Soul Awareness: A Guide's Message,* Gerod describes as "the aspect of your soul which grounds itself in the present physical existence and takes its basis for reality from this particular life."

Here you have had just a taste of Tom and Gerod's work, which has made a great contribution to knowledge. It has been exciting to know Tom. He is a great innovator, a real discoverer. His work in both the exploration and the understanding of consciousness and the treatment of psychological problems is of tremendous value. He is teaching two groups of specially chosen therapists, using Zoom to reach them worldwide. This is a great start, though it is so far ahead of contemporary practice that it is likely to be a long time before Tom's approach is widely used in therapeutic circles.

Tom has not only explored unknown psychological territory, he has also used his own highly organized system of assessing need and designing treatment. He could not have done it without Gerod. This in itself is of great importance, because it is a unique approach to medical exploration and treatment. Before I met Tom and read his first book, my treatment was at a more rudimentary level. Bringing the higher self into the treatment system made it far more effective.

The principal advance that Tom has pioneered is in the concept of an inner world far more complex than anything previously known. This inner world includes spiritual entities and the parts of ourselves known as ego states, which are of great importance for those of us who have intractable problems. Both ego states and spirit attachments have been previously described, but not in the detail that Tom has introduced. It is good to take a long look into the future through Tom's eyes and see it shining.

CHAPTER 6

Lisby's Worldview Changes

A Stolen Harp Sparks Questions

Miracles are not in contradiction to nature. They are only in contradiction with what we know of nature.

SAINT AUGUSTINE (354–430)

I have the joy of bringing many fascinating people to your attention, as I relate how each of them, in different ways, puzzle through anomalous experiences. As you read on, you too may find yourself connecting with the people in a more personal way, just as I do. In this way, we shall all of us gain a closer understanding of what reading can offer our thoughts. In the following account, paraphrased from Elizabeth Lloyd Mayer's book, *Extraordinary Knowing*, Lisby tells of how her worldview changed dramatically when she was able to recover her daughter's stolen harp.

This Changes Everything: The Story of Lisby

First, some background. Elizabeth Lloyd Mayer, "Lisby," was a brilliant psychoanalyst. She inspired colleagues and patients and was never at a loss for creative ideas. She sang contralto for the California Revels, which she founded and directed artistically. Many children and their parents and music teachers have been grateful for Lisby's award-winning video series on music education. She was also a brilliant hockey player. This rainbow of skills paints a unique picture.

Her eleven-year-old daughter, Meg, had a specially made harp, which she played superbly, often performing in public. Following a concert, the harp was stolen. The family was devastated. Lisby tried almost everything—calling the police, calling instrument dealers across the country, posting an ad in the American Harp Society newsletter, even getting a CBS TV news story—to get the harp back. But nothing worked.

Two months later, a valued friend suggested that if she really wanted to get that harp back, she should try calling a dowser. She added that really good dowsers could find lost objects as well as water. People who have the gift of intuitive knowing feel that they obtain their information by entering a state of oneness with the individual or subject of interest.

Lisby took the dare, and her friend gave her the number of Harold McCoy, president of the American Society of Dowsers. She called him, told him the story, and asked if he could help locate it. After a brief pause he told her that the harp was still in Oakland, California, and that if she would send him a street map of Oakland, he would locate the harp. Lisby sent the map and two days later Harold called her back. The harp was on D Street, just off L Avenue, in the second house on the right.

Lisby drove to Oakland, located the house, wrote down the number, and then called the police and told them that she'd had a tip that the harp might be in that house. They refused to act, saying that the information was not good enough for a search warrant and that the harp had probably been sold and left the area. They were closing the case.

Lisby rang off and had a long think. It sounded crazy, but the information wouldn't let her go. She decided to do something about it. She posted flyers in a two-block area around that house. Three days

later the phone rang, and the man on the other end said he'd seen the
flyer. It was exactly the harp his neighbor had recently obtained and
showed him. Two weeks later, after a series of circuitous phone calls,
he told her to meet a teenage boy at 10:00 p.m. in the rear parking
lot of an all-night store. She went. There was a young man loitering in
the lot. Within minutes the harp was in the back of her station wagon
and she drove off.

Twenty-five minutes later, as she turned into her driveway, Lisby
had the thought, "This changes everything." And it did. It changed
how she worked as a clinician and psychoanalyst. It changed the nature
of the research she pursued. "Most of all," she wrote, "it changed my
relatively established, relatively contented, relatively secure sense of
how the world adds up."

She reflected further:

In December of 1991, my daughter's harp was stolen; we got it
back. But it came back in a way that irrevocably changed my familiar world of science and rational thinking. It changed the way I go
about living in that world. It changed the way I perceived the world
and try to make sense of it.

This book is about what unfolded as I attempted to explain what
happened. I encountered questions: huge and disconcerting questions about the world as we know it. They held radical import not
just for science but for the ways we live our everyday lives. This
book is about those questions and some of the surprising answers I
encountered along the way.

Like most of us, Lisby had previously held back from discussing
anomalous incidents, like lost harps that find their owners. Now she
had no choice, because that harp had gone public. It was news. And
once people read the harp story and knew Lisby's secret, they felt
comfortable telling her their stories. There were many shared confi-
dences. One example is a neurosurgeon who told her that he'd stopped

teaching students because he feared sharing the deeper aspects of his work. For instance, he couldn't tell anyone how he would sit with prospective patients until he saw light, the sign that he could operate successfully. When he avoided such subjects in his lectures he was plagued by headaches. Sadly, instead of including this phenomenon to stop the headaches, he chose to avoid teaching altogether.

Lisby did her very best to understand an increasingly challenging world, and she never stopped asking questions. They fizzed around her. She traveled widely and met many scientists and others with whom she discussed anomalies in their areas of interest. The harp turned Lisby's life into an expanded search for meaning. In this, she became a leader. Many others were to benefit from reading her book, and that change continues.

For Lisby, the harp episode was life-turning. She was a strong character, determined and highly intelligent. She had the ability and the means to tread her own path. People needed her skills and they accepted her as she was. She made a change-of-course for which we can be thankful. Her transformation held for fourteen years, until she left for calmer seas on January 1, 2003, dying of natural causes at age fifty-seven. As so often happens with those we need most, Lisby left early. Do you want more about her? Then you will love the ten-minute YouTube video titled "Elizabeth Lloyd Mayer, author of *Extraordinary Knowing.*" In it, Lisby tells her story with zest. This is an anecdote such as today's scientists have been taught to shun. It is subjective and tells things as Lisby experienced them. It is not the usual, lifeless abstraction into which science has converted observations in the service of numerical correctness. Enjoy science lived through the enthusiasm of a true pioneer who devoted her life to the commitment of exploring the unknown. Her story illustrates how our life creates our worldview.

CHAPTER 7

Belief and Knowing

Touching the Truth

The probability that human intelligence developed all the way from the chemical ooze of the primeval ocean solely through sequences of random mechanical processes has been recently aptly compared to the probability of a tornado blowing through a gigantic junkyard and assembling by accident a 747 jumbo jet.

STANISLAV GROF (1931–)

Where is truth? Belief, based on instruction, is one thing, whereas knowing, through subjective experience or objective observation is another. We relate in different ways to the two categories. With exceptions, most personal observations do not have the same powerful influence over us as do group-held beliefs. We internalize the beliefs of religious and materialist faiths and identify with them. This can produce very powerful and persistent attitudes, which may be impervious to opposing evidence. Just to show how difficult some of these decisions are, I'll give some examples:

The Levitation of Daniel Dunglas Home

The medium Daniel Dunglas Home demonstrated that he could levitate. Home proved his "unbelievable" claim when he floated out of one second-floor window (which shocked even him by far exceeding the height of levitations he had done before!) and back through another one. The scientist Sir William Crookes, discoverer of the element thallium, was one of the many people who observed such "unbelievables." Although Crookes did not see Home levitate, he courageously wrote a report in which he confirmed a concertina playing of its own accord in a cage and other "impossibilities." When laughed at by fellow scientists, Crookes famously said, "I didn't say it was possible—I said it was true!"[1]

Looking at it in another way, we can say that, for Crookes, on this occasion, the difference between knowing and believing was the opposite to what I've just stated about group beliefs being more powerful than individual observations. After seeing Home levitate, he was convinced. What about me? Having boldly made a rule, I have just contradicted myself! Conclusion: This is tricky terrain. If one wants to avoid controversy, keep out! But can I? With a swarm of different examples, keeping away can be a problem. There's lots to learn and to enjoy. For Crookes, the difference between knowing and believing was crucial. He didn't just accept that Home could levitate, he knew he could because he actually observed it himself.

According to "common" knowledge such a thing as levitation is impossible. Physicalist science certainly cannot allow it. And when pitted against the enormous reputation of science, how certain can we feel about what we know to be true? Where levitation is concerned, Home is not alone. Michael Grosso's book *The Man Who Could Fly* gives many detailed accounts, witnessed by hundreds and meticulously recorded in the Vatican, of St. Joseph of Cupertino, who levitated on so many occasions that they cannot simply be dismissed. Yet that is precisely what science does. No comment is best.

Another such example is Robert Jahn's experiment in psychokinesis. Whatever the situation, it is well to remember that even scientific theory should be taken with a pinch of thallium.

Proof of Psychokinesis

Robert Jahn, a professor of aerospace science and dean of engineering at Princeton University, took up the challenge to prove that mind can influence matter at a distance. To do this, he designed an objective system that would give the type of numerical results required by science. He used a random-numbers generator with which to investigate the effect of willing a change in the numbers it produced electronically. He invited people to come in off the street, sit near the machine, and wish "high" or "low." This had a small but consistent effect, measured in various ways, such as the number of zeros and ones the machine produced in a given time. Work such as this was continued over an extended period and gave positive results that were billions to one against chance.

Could this really happen? Untrained minds influencing the output of the random-numbers generator?! The implications of the experiment were vast, and the results were widely reported, but there was a problem. They were scientifically "impossible" and therefore must be ignored. No regular scientific journal would accept them. Only the *Journal of Scientific Exploration,* founded to test scientific anomalies, would accept Jahn's submissions. However, ordinary scientists would not read the journal, which was nonphysicalist. The research, supported with ten million dollars from benefactors, lasted from 1979 to 2007. Finally, Jahn gave up on what must surely be one of the most persistent research efforts ever. When asked why he was stopping, Jahn replied that if people did not believe him after twenty-eight years, they never would.

There can be no doubt that both Professor Jahn and physicalist science made powerful statements. Jahn devoted half his life to research that confirmed that mind can influence matter. Science, by ignoring the research results, proclaimed that no observation, however impressive, would be acceptable were it to counter established theory.

Thus, the inability to understand an event—even when it is observed by numerous witnesses—is often taken as a cause to dismiss it. If carefully made observations of an event cannot be explained by current scientific theory, then we need to examine the theory. Science has developed the practice of dismissing what theory cannot explain. That is bad practice, because it neglects essential principles of science, principles of honest thinking, and of observation before speculation.

QUESTIONING BELIEFS

As previously discussed, virtually all religions and spiritual worldviews hold that we survive physical death, after which we exist in another dimension. Scientists mostly hold the opposite view. They say that death is final, with nothing beyond. But is the belief justified?

What we believe about the survival of bodily death and how that belief originated is crucial. Belief is not to be decided only by philosophers, religionists, scientists. Belief is for everybody. We need to look at where beliefs start and how they continue. The beliefs that come from parents, school, or religion are the most persistent. But persistence is not a guide to reliability. Beliefs need testing. But how should we test them?

Scientific beliefs, or theories, based on physicalism are accepted without question. This is natural, but unjustifiable. It is natural to accept what one is taught, especially if it is the first thing. We need to question the apparently profound concept of physicalism that is taught throughout the educational system, more through repetition than through discussion, and simply accepted as truth.

For example, physicalism claims that the universe is made of matter and that the brain creates consciousness, which, for our purpose, we can define as the awareness and ability to consider our thoughts and perceptions. Physicalism cannot be proved, but it can be and has been disproved. For instance, the brain does **not** produce consciousness. This was made evident in chapter 2 when subjects reported veridical experiences that had occurred at times when the brain was totally inactive. (Remember the blue tennis shoe that the unconscious Maria saw on the hospital roof, despite the fact that she had never had an opportunity to see it there, and it was invisible from her body in the hospital ward?)

Total destruction of the brain, on superficial assessment, appears to destroy consciousness permanently. However, we know from countless reincarnation accounts (see chapter 9) that consciousness frequently continues in another body.

It is clear that accepted scientific theory is seriously mistaken, so how can this theory still be accepted? The belief that the brain is responsible for creating all conscious activity persists because it conveniently keeps spiritual questions at bay and keeps them from interfering with other scientific activities. Imagine the embarrassment of admitting that a long-established theory of the revered scientific establishment is utterly wrong!

Of course, even with the self-imposed constraints of physicalism, theories are continually changing. How does change in scientific thinking come about? Let me explain. The term *paradigm* was introduced by Thomas Kuhn in 1963 with his influential book, *The Structure of Scientific Revolutions*. The paradigm that is the system of scientific thought at first makes a strong contribution to knowledge but gradually becomes increasingly influenced by social and educational aspects and eventually becomes a problem that stops the assimilation of new ideas. As the new ideas are finally, suddenly accepted, the existing paradigm has to be abandoned in a process termed scientific revolution. There is a strong feeling now, with so many anomalous phenomena ignored or suppressed, that a paradigm change is necessary. When it comes, after such a long period, the effect will surely be momentous.

No-Touch Spoon Bending

Uri Geller had everyone laughing with his passion for bending spoons, without touch. Spoons the world over bowed to Geller when silently ordered to bend. Geller was, and still is, a world phenomenon. Here's what he did in the presence of Benjamin Netanyahu, the Israeli prime minister, as reported in Annie Jacobsen's book Phenomena: *"Geller stood in one corner of the restaurant and simultaneously bent the spoons of all the people who were there." There were many witnesses. It must have been quite a laugh to see restaurant guests eating soup with bent spoons.*

It doesn't matter if all the spoons were bent, or just some of them, or only one. The fact is that Geller, and others too, are still bending spoons without touch and that science has no answer when asked how it is done. I've no doubt that this feat has been very carefully recorded on many occasions. Of course, photography is fine, but science, with its usual discrimination, prefers not to look. Be it conjuring trick or psychic effect, onlookers were impressed and declared the phenomenon as beyond any normal explanation. My own view is that Geller has psychic abilities, and if he can fascinate millions, when others can only gasp, good luck to him. If my book presents accounts that can be laughed at as well as wondered about, let us be doubly happy!

Geller's spoon bending is an example of psychokinesis, the ability to influence a physical object by thought. Spoon bending made no impression on science. It contradicts theory. Therefore, research on the subject is considered a waste of time.

WHEN BELIEF AND KNOWING COLLIDE

A change in thinking can also happen on an individual level, as it did for me on the topic of UFOs. On a personal note, I must say that UFOs gave me a lot of pain recently, as I took my morning walk through the local nature reserve. I had spent a day reading Leslie Kean's well-researched book *UFOs: Generals, Pilots, and Government Officials Go on the Record* and felt immensely unsettled. My worldview was drowning in incompatible material. My brain longed for an instant change, but the vivid descriptions and pictures and the reports of observing authorities could not be dismissed.

The result was a most uncomfortable headache, unlike anything I had experienced. It lasted for half an hour, and no attempt at diversion could get rid of it. My attitudes and beliefs, established early in my life, were protesting at the enormity of the UFO images, even though I had accepted them intellectually.

UFOs were not fitting in with my customary beliefs, but they could not simply be dismissed. How could one read about observations made by thousands, including pilots, senior police, military members, and many others of incontestable authority, without at least considering their authenticity?

The 1982 Hudson Valley wave of UFO sightings involved repeated visits by huge, silent objects, sometimes more than one at a time, hovering at low altitudes with extremely bright spotlights. Observers said these structures appeared to be as large as football fields and were capable of shooting off, silently, at incredible speeds from stationary positions. Thousands were convinced. Impossible? Yes! At least according to the "laws" of science and the denials of the US military. And yet we know that the scientific certainties that control our thinking are never permanent.

I write about my headache because just thinking of these incompatibilities hurt horribly. I went for a walk and tried to distract myself by examining leaves, watching birds, and talking to strangers. Nothing helped. The discomfort ruined my walk. It only stopped when, back home, I took a dirty carpet outside to beat it! What does that mean? It illustrates my difficulty in simultaneously holding incompatible thoughts: the difference between my early beliefs and the growing evidence leading me toward knowing. Psychologists call this cognitive dissonance. I thought back to when using hypnosis with my patients and being able to make contact with attached spirits changed my thinking completely. I went beyond accepted belief to personal observations, where I could say, "I know." So perhaps the only cure for this painful dissonance process is to personally observe or come into contact with UFOs or extraterrestrials and know that they truly exist. Since the United States recently admitted that the UFO information had been suppressed, this may happen sooner rather than later.

CHAPTER 8

Hypnosis

Mesmer Awakens the Subconscious

Hypnosis has an exciting image and an intriguing history. I write of it here because I used hypnosis as an introduction to spiritual work with my patients.

While not everyone can enter a hypnotic trance, most people can do so with persistence. What is more, those who need hypnotherapy are usually better able to achieve a hypnotic trance than are the non-needy. There are many ways of inducing trance. I usually began with muscle relaxation with eyes closed. This was followed by opening the eyes to look at an imaginary spot on the ceiling. When my patients' eyes tired and closed, I would have them visualize walking down steps to a bench in a sun-blessed garden. Then I would deepen the trance, as necessary.

When asked specifically for help with attached spirits, I might ask my patient to look in an imaginary mirror or to imagine the body filled with light, and I might ask questions such as "Is anyone there who is not part of Mary?" If there were no verbal responses, I would induce finger signals—one finger for yes, another finger for no, and a hand movement for don't know. The accounts of spirit release in chapter 3 showed the progression that occurred after making contact with part of the subconscious mind or an attached spirit.

Another reason for writing this chapter is that hypnosis, especially "magnetism," as the condition became known in the 1770s, can introduce those scientifically impossible white crows. I believe this is a reason why hypnosis, despite repeated demonstrations of its efficacy in treating many forms of psychological and medical problems, has never been readily accepted as a mode of treatment. There are too many unknowns.

Most people are familiar with the term *mesmerized,* used to describe a sense of being put into a state of awe or wonder. The word comes from the name of Dr. Franz Mesmer, whose treatment was famous throughout Europe in the 1770s and for much of the next century.

Franz Anton Mesmer studied philosophy, theology, and law before qualifying in medicine at the age of thirty-three, with a dissertation on the influence of the planets on human illness. Upon qualifying, he married a wealthy widow. They lived in Vienna on a splendid estate that included an opera house, where they invited Mozart, aged twelve, to stage his first opera. Mesmer, himself a musician, played the glass harmonica, which he used in his treatments. Mozart wrote a piece for the harmonica, which is now available on the internet, perhaps for Mesmer, who knows? Here follows one of his stories.

Magnetism Is Both Cause and Cure

In 1774, Mesmer's medical focus changed when he used magnets, a recent discovery, in his treatment of Francisca, a young woman whose complaints had resisted all other treatments. Placing magnets on her legs and abdomen, he had her swallow iron filings to provoke an "artificial tide." Soon she began to feel streams of mysterious fluid running through her body and she was freed from her symptoms for some hours. It took several months of Mesmer's treatment before Francisca could regain her health and return home. She celebrated the event by marrying Mesmer's stepson.

The cure convinced Mesmer that he had discovered a completely new principle in medical treatment. Although he credited the magnets with the success of Francisca's treatment, he believed that the magnetic streams were produced by an invisible fluid in his own body, which he called "animal magnetism." There were other remarkable successes, both before and after Francisca's, in which Mesmer's ability as a healer created an immediate effect. His enthusiasm for this idea knew no bounds. He was convinced that animal magnetism was a universal dimension, responsible for both cause and cure. "There is only one illness and one healing," he would say.

Mesmer's major intuition was that not only he but every human being was the bearer of animal magnetism. He believed that a universal, impersonal energy could be stored in people, objects, or places and could be known through its objective effects. Mesmer devoted all his energies to developing this theory, which he felt could open the door to a new epoch in the treatment of illness. This aim set him on a collision course with every doctor in Europe and ensured a constant state of conflict with organized medicine.

In 1777, Mesmer moved to Paris. Influential helpers soon had him installed in a mansion in the center of the city, where he was besieged by the needy and the curious in crowds. Judging from the behavior of his patients, who extolled his treatments and paid him enormous sums for them, to be mesmerized was a unique healing experience. To satisfy the demand, Mesmer devised group treatment methods, such as mesmerizing trees with longitudinal passes along the trunk. Ropes were attached to the branches, so that people could hold them to experience animal magnetism. He placed in the house circular wooden containers called *baquets,* where up to twenty people might sit and connect with "electrolyzed" water and with each other.

These group treatments were often successful. This accords well with the finding that suggestion can be especially effective when groups of people are being treated together. An English visitor recorded that, throughout the day, there were never fewer than two hundred people seeking treatment in Mesmer's Parisian mansion.

This was a stressful time for Mesmer, not least because he was constantly in touch with influential people who were trying to extend his work even further. This intensive period lasted five years and ended with the pronouncements of two official bodies set up to investigate mesmerism. Much to Mesmer's disappointment, though they did not deny that the treatment was effective, they concluded that there was no evidence that animal magnetism was the effective principle involved. Mesmer was devastated. He left Paris and disappeared from public view. Although his work was continued by many others, he had failed to bring about the medical revolution that he had dreamed of.

The outcome demonstrates that the medical profession will scarcely ever accept a new treatment unless it is supported by a theory that has already been agreed upon and confirmed. That keeps us safe, you might think. But it means that beneficial change can be delayed for a long time. Even though his theory was flawed, Mesmer's methods were a great stimulus to develop new treatments and in increasing knowledge of the subconscious mind.

During the Paris period, Mesmer had been actively training individuals to use his method, so when he left, there were many who were qualified to continue his work. One person in particular not only continued but extended Mesmer's legacy, though in a much less flamboyant style. This was Armand Marie Jacques de Chastenet, Marquis de Puysegur, a distinguished general who survived the Revolution of 1789 and left a well-ordered collection of writings on what he termed "artificial somnambulism."

Magnetic Sleep Engenders Two States of Consciousness

When Puysegur used the magnetic passes that Mesmer had taught him to help Victor Race, a laborer on his estate, the effect surprised him. Victor fell asleep after a few minutes, but it was an unusual sleep in which he responded very differently from Puysegur's expectations. While Victor was in the magnetized state, his intelligence and general mental alertness improved greatly. Another remarkable finding was that Victor was aware of Puysegur's thoughts without any words being spoken. The rapport was such that no one other than Puysegur could touch Victor without causing him extreme agitation.

The most remarkable aspect of "magnetic sleep," as Puysegur termed the condition, was that Victor displayed two very different states of consciousness. The original Victor had no awareness of what had happened while he had been asleep, whereas a different Victor, who had taken over during the magnetism, seemed to be much more intelligent and had a clear idea of everything that had happened. It was as if Puysegur was dealing with two different people. Puysegur's discovery was widely confirmed by others and received much attention throughout Europe. It is here that we touch on dissociative identity disorder, a fascinating and highly complex subject that is still much neglected.

Magnetism was also used to perform painless surgery, and impressive examples were demonstrated by two British doctors, John Elliotson and James Esdaile, in the 1840s. Esdaile published accounts of hundreds of major operations he performed painlessly in India. This was just before the introduction in the 1850s of anesthetics. Chemical anesthetics won on ease of application and predictability.

Silent passes over the patient's recumbent body, as used by mesmerists, or magnetizers as practitioners were often called, have been replaced by spoken inductions in hypnosis as practiced today. This is due to the influence of James Braid, a Scottish physician who, in 1842, modified the technique and named it hypnosis. Why verbal and suggestive techniques took over is unclear. Perhaps induction by silent passes with eyes closed is more than most people can believe. But magnetism is undoubtedly the procedure to use for animals, as is described and photographed in detail by Ferenc Andras Volgyesi in his book *Hypnosis of Man and Animals*.

Research on telepathic hypnosis has also been done. Here's an example as reported by Dr. Dusart in the *Tribune Medicale* in May 1875.

Silent Commands Are Effective Even at a Distance

Dr. Dusart found that one of his subjects, a "hysterical"* girl of fourteen, was very susceptible to hypnotism. He had earlier remarked that his passes were ineffective if his attention was not strongly directed to the desired result. He therefore tried the effect of a purely mental direction. One day, before the usual hour for waking the patient had arrived, he gave her the silent mental command to awake. The effect was instantaneous. Dusart found that he could also put his patient to sleep from a distance, even when she was unaware of his intention.

More than one hundred experiments of the sort were performed under various conditions but with uniform success. On one occasion Dusart gave the order mentally, at a distance of seven kilometers, and found that it had been punctually obeyed. He repeated the experiment several times, at different hours, and each time was successful.

Readers, I hope you enjoyed reading about hypnosis. Remote hypnosis is certainly a white crow. Skeptics would have to turn to philosopher David Hume, who dismissed "miracles" by asking, Which is more likely, that witnesses should tell lies or that the laws of nature should be violated? Long before I started to write this book my faith in the "laws of nature" was more than shaky. In the matter of remote hypnosis, my vote goes to Dr. Dusart.

---

*The term *hysterical* is no longer a medical diagnosis. Emotionally unstable and highly suggestible, though not an official diagnosis, is preferable.

CHAPTER 9

Reincarnation

Change Promotes Growth

How do I know who I am or where I am? How could a single wave locate itself in an ocean?

RUMI (1207–1273)

There was a time when reincarnation took no part in my thinking. Then it happened: I met a Roman soldier from two thousand years ago!

With hypnosis, a direct instruction can often have a striking effect. In 1993, I was using hypnosis with a depressed and anxious electrician. "Go back to the start of your problem," I said. That took him back, not to a trauma in this life, but to a much earlier time of which he had no prior knowledge in this lifetime. My patient went back two thousand years to when he was a Roman soldier dying in a desperate battle. How could a very ordinary individual who had no historical interests change so dramatically to another character completely different from anything he had ever knowingly thought or felt? TV, you may suppose, had sown the seed. Possibly, but there was no conscious connection. The scene seemed real and the emotions genuine. Somehow, we felt, it must really have happened. The session was a powerful experience for both of us. That was the day when, for me, reincarnation came alive because

I had observed it firsthand, just as William Crookes witnessed Daniel Dunglas Home levitating.

I was excited as I drove home that evening. I needed to tell someone, "Reincarnation is a reality!" The Sri Lankan night porter opened the gate to me. "Nianzu," I blurted, "do you believe in reincarnation?" "Of course!" he beamed. "It is the voice of truth." Nianzu's Buddhist certainty buttressed my therapy experience.

Now for some additional evidence. For millennia religions have been the only voices on reincarnation. Hindus and Buddhists place reincarnation at the center of their belief systems. Christians, Muslims, and Jews are of the one-life-only view. The dogmas are fixed. Reincarnation had been part of early Christian teaching but was excluded by the Roman emperor Justinian, in 553 CE at the Second Council of Constantinople, which the pope refused to attend and at which there was an unrepresentative sample of bishops. It seems tragic that through largely political reasons Christianity should have been deprived of a teaching that could have given it a far more comprehensive perspective on life.

For physicalist scientists, reincarnation is a fantasy, since they see no survival beyond physical death. Behind the scenes, the situation is changing rapidly. In the past sixty years consistent research has revealed convincing evidence that humans survive physical death and are often, though not invariably, reborn. Not only that, but between incarnations, there is a disembodied stage, which we shall come to shortly.

What does the research show, as far as we can read it? It seems that most of us have repeated incarnate and discarnate experiences. The incarnate lives seem to be mostly on Earth; the discarnate periods are mostly in another dimension. In this chapter, we'll start with reincarnation, which has been illuminated by two different approaches: spontaneous recollection and hypnotic regression.

SPONTANEOUS RECOLLECTION
OF REINCARNATION

Research into children's spontaneous recollection of past lives, which usually fades before they are six, began in 1960 with Ian Stevenson, professor of psychiatry at the University of Virginia, whose meticulous work lasted forty years. Stevenson traveled widely, focusing particularly on areas where there was a belief in reincarnation, such as India, Sri Lanka, Myanmar, and Alaska. Together with associated researchers, Stevenson recorded more than 2,500 cases, in two-thirds of which a previous person was identified whose life matched, to a greater or lesser degree, the statements that the child made.

A significant aspect of these children's recollections is that about 70 percent of them had died violently in events such as murder, accident, or suicide. Many of them had marks on their bodies corresponding to the described mode of death. For instance, in death by shooting, there was commonly a small mark indicating the entry point and a larger mark indicating the exit wound. The fact that we do not understand the mechanism of such findings does not disprove the connection. It simply indicates our ignorance. Professor Stevenson's reincarnation research gives overwhelming support for the belief that we survive death.

On meeting their claimed relatives, these children commonly identified them with great certainty, recalling their pet names and other aspects of behavior. They spoke convincingly of experiences within the family and identified objects of which they could not otherwise have known. This was impressive and convincing to Stevenson and other investigators. Stevenson believed that research on reincarnation had particular relevance as proof of survival.

The following is a dramatic case of spontaneous recollection of reincarnation and a perfect example of "white-crowness." It is an amazing story in which many detailed claims are listed and upheld. The case has been thoroughly researched and described with great knowledge and understanding by Leslie Kean in two chapters of her book *Surviving Death*. Her account follows many interviews with the father, Bruce Leininger, and includes a chapter by Dr. Jim Tucker, the child psychiatrist and reincarnation specialist, now the successor to Ian Stevenson at the University of Virginia, who met James and advised the parents.

Spontaneous Recall (Aged Two Years) of Death as Fighter Pilot

James Leininger was born in 1998 and two years later was reliving his death in 1945, as James Huston, in his burning warplane, fighting the Japanese.

The story began in May 2000. James was not quite two years old. His father took him to the Cavanaugh Flight Museum, near Dallas. James III, as he later named himself, had never seen World War II airplanes before. He greeted them with peals of delight and for three hours resisted his dad's attempts to get him away from the scene. Several weeks later his mother gave James a plastic airplane, indicating the "bomb" under the fuselage. He corrected her, saying, "That's not a bomb, Mommy. It's a drop tank."

James III knew it, despite never having seen such a plane, much less drop tanks made to supply extra fuel for long flights. Following this event, James was obsessed with World War II planes. He played with them continuously, repeatedly crashing them against the coffee table to destroy the propellers.

James was little more than two when the nightmares started. Still deeply asleep, he screamed, thrashing wildly. This happened most nights, causing his parents great concern. A pediatrician could offer no solution. Later, Dr. Jim Tucker explained to Bruce and Andrea that little children often play out their problems with dramas of past events, as James did when, again and again, he fell from a toy cockpit at home, as might a pilot attempting to parachute. James also did hundreds of drawings of warring planes in post-traumatic play.

Often, during dreams, James would scream, "Airplane crash on fire! Little man can't get out!"

One evening, as Andrea read a book to him, James, aged only two, said he was little man. His plane, flying from the USS Natoma Bay, was shot down by the Japanese.

Bruce, an evangelical Christian, found his worldview threatened. Saving it was his priority. He commented later, "I was convinced that I somehow had to trap James to find the cracks or flaws in his story." He worked tirelessly on the internet to understand and solve the problem. Gradually, as with a jigsaw, the missing bits appeared, though often not as he had hoped. Some findings had special significance. James spoke of Jack Larsen, also a pilot. Larsen was located, and James's statements were confirmed. Another key fact came to light one day as James sat on his dad's knee, looking at The Battle for Iwo Jima, a book that Bruce had bought for his father. Seeing a photo of Iwo Jima, James said, "Daddy, that's when my plane was shot down and crashed."

Bruce found records confirming that the Natoma Bay was there during the battle. Only one of its planes was shot down on March 3, 1945. It was flown by James Huston Jr. Andrea saw the significance of "Jr." Immediately. It made sense of her son often calling himself James III.

James also had memories that seemed to come from events occurring between death and rebirth. He told his parents, "When I found you and Mommy, I knew you would be good to me." When asked for details, James said that his mom and dad were at a big pink hotel in Hawaii: "I found you on the beach. You were eating dinner at night."

Bruce confirmed this, saying that they had eaten dinner on the beach on their last night there. This was five weeks before Andrea learned she was pregnant. A disembodied earth experience occurring between death and rebirth is known as an "intermission memory." Another intermission memory concerned three G.I. Joe dolls, which

James was given and took to bed each night. He gave them the names of three Natoma Bay pilots: Billy, Leon, and Walter, who had died in 1944. When asked why he had used these names, he said matter-of-factly, "Because that's who met me when I got to heaven."

Of the many details that James gave, only one appeared to be a mistake. When Bruce asked the type of plane he flew, James said, "Corsair." He had never seen a Corsair; there were none at the Cavanaugh Flight Museum, and no Corsairs had flown from the Natoma Bay. This was a cause of hope for Bruce that the story was fabrication. Finally, even this passed the test. Searching through James Huston's details, Bruce found that he had flown a Corsair for a while, from another aircraft carrier, before joining Natoma Bay.

There are more details, but the chief facts are clear. What I want to stress now is how difficult it was for Bruce to accept what his son was saying. Bruce told it as follows:

In a funny way this made me mad. He wasn't even potty-trained, and he was telling me something that shook my world. I was venturing into truly unknown territory. I began to panic, quietly. My wife and her family wondered about a possible "past life." I told them, "Not in my house!" I needed to be right about this. My spiritual side was ruled by the Christian faith, which did not accept reincarnation.

The more I learned from James, the stronger my mission became to prove that the nightmares and everything else were simply the coincidental rants of a child.* I was hardened into a committed skeptic. I had to represent the voice of reason within the family.[1]

Bruce's words show very clearly the power of belief. Losing his beliefs must have felt almost like an amputation.

---

*Reading the words "coincidental rants of a child," one must sympathize with children under school age whose claims of past lives are confidently dismissed by "knowledgeable" parents. Even in these enlightened times such children can't have one chance in ten of being taken seriously.

Now we come to another aspect of reincarnation, with a totally different manifestation: hypnotic regression.

HYPNOTIC REGRESSION TO PREVIOUS EARTH LIVES

Hypnosis can be used to regress the individual to a previous life. This is usually in search of hidden trauma that has caused problems in the present life, but it may also be used as a research procedure or simply for personal interest.

The following case of past-life regression through hypnosis has impressive confirmatory information and comes from the YouTube video "This Life, Past Life" by Keith Parsons, who is known for his YouTube presentations on psychic phenomena and afterlife knowledge.

Regression to the Crimean War

Ray Bryant was a journalist on the Reading Evening Post *in the 1980s. He decided to write some articles on past lives and agreed to be hypnotized by the regression expert Joe Keeton. "It's rather like watching yourself on film," writes Ray. "You are in the film and watching it at the same time. It's a very strange dream-like state and you're aware of the dream, so you can follow it. You know what's happening all the time."*

One life that Ray recalled was his life as a soldier in the Crimean War of 1853 to 1856. The trouble was, he couldn't remember his full name. He knew it was Reuben Sta . . . , but he couldn't complete that surname. Keeton decided to investigate the matter on his behalf. Fortunately, the Public Record Office at Kew in London yielded a complete list of the men who had fought in the Crimean War. Among them was a Reuben Stafford. So, under hypnosis, and without telling Ray what was discovered, Keeton asked him the significance of the names of various English towns—Manchester, Sheffield, Nottingham, Stafford. When he heard the name of the town of Stafford, Ray was able to confirm that it was his surname in his former life.

That was a breakthrough, because in the meantime the researchers had discovered the entire military record of Reuben Stafford, including his wounds, his promotion to sergeant, his pay rise, when he was demobilized, and, from other sources, the cause and date of his death.

Without prompting, and despite trick questions to put him off the trail, Ray Bryant, under hypnosis, was able accurately to answer questions about the life of Reuben Stafford. The case was visually recorded, so Ray Bryant was seen, under hypnosis reliving the day he was wounded in his former life.

Ray: Forward! (heavy breathing) Forward! For-forward! (breathing pace increases) Mm-mm (apparent pain).
Joe Keeton: Off to sleep! Sleep, Reuben! Sleep. Sleep, Reuben. Sleep, Reuben.
Ray Bryant relaxes.

After Reuben Stafford left the army, his life went downhill. Following sundry misfortunes, he became depressed. He was working as a waterman on the River Thames at Millwall in East London. Under hypnosis, Ray Bryant relives his death as he drowned off the quayside at Millwall Dock. In the video he sputters and chokes until Joe Keeton instructs him again to go off to sleep.

When Ray returned from hypnosis, he was in for a big shock. Never knowing that his memories were real, because the researchers had kept from him what they knew about Reuben Stafford, he was amazed to be given his own copy of his death certificate from that former life. His past-life recall was factually correct.

That death certificate from the UK's General Register Office shows the following:

Reuben Stafford died, aged 52. He was a waterman, suffered a violent death—suffocation by drowning—and he was found on 2nd April 1879 in the waters off Millwall Dock.

Not many cases of past-life regression are so well documented.

The next example is from Dr. Edith Fiore's book *You Have Been Here Before: A Psychologist Looks at Past Lives*. Dr. Fiore tells me that this case is her favorite. Despite having to shorten it, I have retained the admirable essence. The full account can be read in the original publication, which contains many more fascinating accounts by this master therapist.

A Past-Life Murder Is the Key to a Cure

Elizabeth had suffered all her life from severe depression and anxiety. She had seen psychiatrists and taken antidepressants and tranquilizers, with little effect.

"Somehow, I know these anxieties have been carried over from past lives, I can't allow myself to make a mistake. I've felt guilty all my life."

Several years before, she was drawn into a very deep depression that lasted for three years. She was slipping into the same pattern again and it scared her. Shuddering, Elizabeth said that she couldn't bear seeing anything violent or destructive. Even the slightest amount of blood revolted her. Of her many anxieties, by far the most crippling was a terror of coming home and finding her three children, now teenagers, knifed to death. On the few outings she had with her husband, she insisted, on their return, that he go and check on the children. She would only leave the car when he had done so.

It took many sessions before Dr. Fiore was able to induce finger signals for "yes," "no," and "I don't want to answer." Finally, a dream brought the solution. Elizabeth had spoken earlier about a recurring dream of entering a beautiful Victorian house. Every dream took her knowledge of that house a little further, but she never saw upstairs. Now came a dream of another house that felt somehow better, but there was still a terrifying unexplored room.

Dr. Fiore has Elizabeth continue the dream in hypnosis:

[Elizabeth:] 'The word "murder," just flashed through my mind.' Next came "red, knife, curls, little girl's nightie, a farm."

Elizabeth, then Sarah, is in the kitchen of a small farmhouse. She is helping to get her sister-in-law's three children ready for bed. There's to be a party in the village that night. Sarah wants to go, but the sister-in-law decides to stay home with the children. When Sarah returns home, the house is in darkness. The expected candle is not burning.

[Elizabeth:] 'The bedroom door is shut. I can't open that door. (crying) I've got to open that door . . . I'm standing in front of that door . . . I'm so scared . . . there isn't a sound anywhere! I know I opened that door. Why can't I open that door now?'

Dr. Fiore (taking her hand and stroking it): "You're not alone. I'm here with you. Open the door and tell me what you see."

With much encouragement Sarah finally opens it and sees carnage. Could it have been her brother? He was always a violent man, but nothing like this. Sarah manages to walk five miles to the sheriff's house to report the tragedy. She never gets over it and ends her life in a psychiatric hospital.

[Dr Fiore:] 'Now I'm going to ask you to remember this when you wake up. It's very important for this to be part of your conscious mind. Know that you have opened the attic door, haven't you? You've uncovered all the horrors deep within you that have kept you feeling so anxious when you're away from your children . . . and when you come back at night. Do you understand now why it was hard for you to have a good time either at a party or away from them? Afraid that when you came back that they'd be stabbed . . . remember when we talked about that?'

There was much more in the same vein. Dr. Fiore then asked if the brother and the children were present in this lifetime. Elizabeth says the brother is her frighteningly violent father in this life and the children are her own children. Dr. Fiore asked her not to tell the children but to share her regression with her husband to be sure none of it became repressed again, even though she seemed to handle it well once she got it out. Then she suggested Elizabeth make a list of all the ways her life as Sarah had affected her in this lifetime.

At the next session, Elizabeth was smiling broadly. She wore a cheery Indian-print sundress.

'I feel great! It worked! Chris and I went to that show in San Francisco. I had a good time. And I didn't worry at all about the children. I walked right in when we got home, before I realized what I had done.'

They discussed the treatment from different aspects. As she left, Elizabeth said,

'I'm still flabbergasted at how simple it's been!'

Here's Dr. Fiore's original final paragraph of an account that richly repays reading:

It has been almost six months since Elizabeth's first session. Working with her has been challenging, exciting, suspenseful, and extremely rewarding for me. I have thoroughly enjoyed watching—and helping—her dreams unfold.[2]

Fear of death is widespread, but it rarely reaches the degree seen in the following case of my patient Merlin.

Death Phobia Relieved
by Reincarnation Regression

Merlin's death phobia was so great that it affected his whole life. Even the sight of his naked body scared him, since he feared that he would see signs of a fatal illness. As he put it, "Seeing [these signs] would bring me back to my thanatophobia [fear of death]. I avoided going to medical appointments or medically themed TV programs or other media that might trigger a response. I also avoided looking in mirrors, showered with the light off, and couldn't have my photograph taken."

Merlin achieved a degree in engineering with extreme difficulty because of obsessive-compulsive symptoms. Subsequently, he managed intermittent employment with the support of his psychologist wife. A therapist referred Merlin to me with suspected spirit possession, but the heart of the problem turned out to be past-life trauma, which became evident through the help of a healing spirit who spoke to me while Merlin was in hypnosis. The spirit knew what was needed, and Merlin was soon reliving a series of battle scenes from hundreds of years earlier. Reexperiencing those deaths freed Merlin from hidden memories, and the effect lasted.

I kept in touch with Merlin and was delighted to find, ten years after treatment, his fear was greatly diminished. I emailed him my description of his case. Here is his helpful reply: "I have recently been working in a morgue and have never felt more alive. Yes, I still have questions about life and where I am going, but after such a long and painful delay my journey of discovery has well and truly started. I have freedom."

Three years after that response, Merlin had lived through the Covid-19 pandemic. In April 2021, he wrote,

It was a very interesting experience for me, after living in the fear of death for so long, suddenly to witness such a collective fear in the wider society. The effort that I had put in to try to understand my old foe death had given me the tools, missing in others, to deal with this existential crisis.

Experience from a previous life can have profound effects on later incarnations. For parents with young children, spontaneous recollection of past lives is something to think of, especially if your child expresses much upset at an early age. The pediatrician consulted by the Leiningers had nothing to offer. This is to be expected, since past lives are not yet part of current medical training. Despite the intensity of James's experiences, the father, steeped in his religious training, could not believe that the dreams were based on reality. Only when lengthy investigations had confirmed every one of James's claims could Bruce accept the truth of his son's story.

What a story it is! What a confirmation! We, along with Bruce, have to ask ourselves, How could it not be true?

Here is veridical information that cannot be accounted for in any other way.

Contemporary science makes no attempt to counter these findings. It simply maintains that, according to physicalist theory, the brain produces consciousness and death ends everything. It considers this self-evident. No evidence is offered.

Physicalist science ignores relevant research, despite the overwhelming confirmation of reincarnation. Even more damning than the lack of contrary evidence is the lack of will to examine the question. For me, the case for reincarnation is conclusive.

CHAPTER 10

Messages through a Medium
Teachings from the Afterlife

Afterlife or interlife, which should it be? We're at the in-between stage, so far as this question goes. I prefer interlife, since, for me, reincarnation is well established, but afterlife is more commonly used. I shall be using both terms, especially when quoting other works. It may be helpful to think of your many incarnations as a personal video gallery in which each repeated life experience has its own monitor, but all except the current life are draped in a black cloth. Each screen contains a video with all the activity of that life. If all of the monitors are covered, the individual will be between lives, known as the afterlife.

Information about the afterlife comes from mediumistic work of various sorts. The spirit may speak either to or through the medium, or it may communicate by automatic writing or even through hypnosis, as in Michael Newton's work, which we'll look at in chapter 11. An excellent publication, *The Afterlife Unveiled* by Stafford Betty gives seven fascinating and highly varied accounts from mediums who transmit their experiences.

The afterlife is a mysterious place. It is said to have many layers, with different properties. Some accounts tell of a world somewhat like our Earth but differing in many particulars. For instance, buildings have no roofs and there is always light, though not from our sun. Our bodies differ too. There is no need to eat or drink or void waste or even to sleep. We can travel instantly, at will. This is lower-level stuff. At a higher level, there is no body or apparent surroundings. Those of us who consult mediums in the hope of speaking with a recently deceased relative will find them at a low level. It takes time to progress. How can we understand these striking differences?

We may not be able to understand the situation until we leave this Earth and remember why these things are the way they are. We would not expect a fish to understand what goes on above the surface. It might know some things, such as other fish being caught by an angler from the riverbank. Other events, such as what goes on in football games or on airplanes, would be beyond its concern. For now, it is quite sufficient for our purposes to know of the Leininger story, the near-death experiences, and the many other events that demonstrate beyond a doubt that consciousness can occur, at times, without an active brain or body.

Here is a simplified outline of the two worlds we live in, the worlds in which we develop as individuals. One world is our amazing Mother Earth, which provides a testing environment in which we face the many endurances, loves, responsibilities, and disasters that make our earth life such a perfect challenge. Another world is made up of the many levels beyond bodily experience, which are described in mediumistic texts. The chief difference between the two worlds is the degree of responsiveness. Beyond the earthly experience, plants grow and blossom as we wish, our house is moved or fashioned as we watch, thoughts are freely known to others without a word, and in no time we can be anywhere with just a thought.

So where are heaven and hell, the concepts we know so well from religious teaching? The view that comes from mediumistic accounts is that hell is not a place but a spiritual state of being in which conditions continue to take effect until the soul reaches the decision to really change. This may take a very long time. To illustrate the torment of self-imposed hell, here is an extract, from automatic writing, of Air Chief Marshall Lord Dowding's book *Lychgate: The Entrance to the Path,* in which a Nazi soldier, Franz, tells of his state after death and how he was affected because of his part in World War II atrocities.

Hell Is a Self-Imposed State

I was very young when Hitler took me from my parents and forced me to accept his way of life. It was fine, of course, to be told you are little less than God and that your lightest wish may be answered if only you follow the Leader. Then came the War and I was sent to Poland, and on to Norway and then to France. At first, I was triumphant; then success seemed too easy and it palled; then it began to sicken me and I saw these conquered peoples had what we had not—Love and Unselfishness and the power to endure under our rule—and it sickened me to be sent to kill and bayonet them and harry the old and the sick. My soul was sick with horror and blood and at last I refused to go on and was myself shot by my own comrades. That is all my story, but now the worst comes.

I had no one to meet me or to help me. I was alone in the torture and torment that never ceased, a torment of the mind. I could not turn my thoughts to other things as I had done in life. I was obsessed by the crimes and horrors I had committed and those whom I had hurt came to me, showing me their wounds and I was hopeless and helpless and beyond any expression I was damned.

So this is the end to which our vain boastings bring us. I saw it clearly and longed to show others but it was no use; I couldn't speak or move. I was so weak from the misery; all my strength seemed to go in the agony of enduring this mental torture of my past life.

Then light broke. The child I had been told to kill or wound was killed by another when I refused and she bore witness for me that I had done one good thing; I had refused to kill her, and in doing so I had lost my own life. This came as a tiny light in the darkness through which I struggled, and then some of my own family long since dead, were able to come to me, but they were horrified by the blood through which I had waded and only came near enough to see me; they were shocked that I should have fallen so low, and were not proud of me as a Conqueror or One of the Herrenvolk whom I was always told to revere. I was miserable; there seemed to be no hope; if I climbed towards the Light it only illuminated the loathsomeness of the ME that had survived. . . .

You can never know how much we suffer or how vastly we expiate our sins through suffering of intense bitterness.

FRANZ VON EITELMANRT[1]

Dowding records speaking of Franz in a lecture in September 1943, while the war was still raging. A seer described the scene, telling how Franz's spirit stood next to Dowding as he spoke. At the climax, he joined a group of spirits who had been English airmen, where he was well received. The culmination came when the audience sang "Land of Hope and Glory." A second letter by automatic writing came from Franz soon after the meeting. In it, he said, "I see it all now, our mistakes and broken promises and the results they entail. Thank you. I see the way now. I am upon firm ground. You have given me back hope and companionship. I live again."

AFTERLIFE TEACHERS

One of the joys of writing is the pleasure of introducing, among the different subjects, some of the teachers themselves. William James, Elizabeth Mayer, and Franz Mesmer have already visited, and there are more to come.

Frances Banks and Alvin Daniel (A. D.) Mattson, were great teachers from the afterlife. Both led productive religious lives, and each of them made it clear that they would do their best to give further information after they had passed to the afterlife. I'll start with Frances Banks, for whom I have the luxury of two accounts to guide me, *Testimony of Light,* the posthumous account by Helen Greaves, and Frances's own *Frontiers of Revelation,* written shortly before her death. She is on the move and I must catch her coattails as best I can.

Frances Banks Makes Contact from the Other Side

"See you in the next world!"

This was the uncommon greeting from Frances to the doctor who cared for her in a London hospital in those closing days. Frances was an uncommon person. She refused analgesia for terminal cancer and had her own way of handling the transition.

"Am I still here? I had hoped to have gone."

Although keen to move on, she saw her departure as an opportunity to take on a new role with greater responsibilities.

It took a little while for Frances to make the change, but once she did, her intimate friend, Helen Greaves, with whom she had studied meditation and telepathy for the previous eight years, was waiting and hoping. One evening, about three weeks after Frances's death, Helen gradually became aware of her. Helen was alone when, slowly, her whole being became caught up in an indescribable sense of peace and beauty, and she passed into a state of deep meditation in which she felt herself to be immersed in light and in communication, at a soul level, with Frances. The experience lasted half an hour.

Some days later, they were again in communication. Helen wrote,

Words dropped into my thoughts did not come from my consciousness.

Helen knew that they were linked in telepathic communication. She began to write. "Words, thoughts, sentences, tumbled out onto the paper. It was almost as if I took dictation." This was not automatic writing, because she was in control and fully conscious. She wrote for an hour, continuously. Periods of such writing continued for days. Frances explained that she was under the instruction of a group to give material for a book.

Frances began her account by describing surroundings in her "rest home," from which she looked out onto a rolling plain and sunlit hills. She was accompanied by Mother Florence, a past Mother Superior of the order, and other colleagues who had gone on ahead. As Frances became aware of her new situation, she was also able to have an awareness of earth friends in Maidstone Prison and at Exeter Cathedral, where they gathered to honor her passing. She was filled with elation at the knowledge that she could "tune in" and see the earth plane if her desire was strong enough. At the London memorial service, she felt that she was able to make her presence known, a feeling that Helen later confirmed.

With Mother Florence and other previous colleagues, Frances discussed her situation and how she might use her psychological expertise in her new role. She also spent much time in reviewing her earth life and how she had sometimes achieved far less than she had thought at the time. She saw "blueprints" contrasting how she behaved and how things could have been. At first, during this comparison, she felt alone, but later she had someone beside her to help. Whether this was her own "High Spirit" or a "Great Helper," she was uncertain. This was a wonderful experience that brought understanding and tranquility. She was preparing to help others who had gotten "stuck."

"I must tell you about my garden. You remember the secret place of our meditations? . . . I thrill when I see some of the results."

There were many visitors. One man had been brutal and bitter to his wife and family. Now he felt tied to the people on whom he had exercised his cruelty and bitterness. Frances showed him her garden. He spent time there and begged to come again. There were many needing help, some of whom were in a far worse state than this man, and Frances explained the value of her work to Helen.

She made friends with a brilliant surgeon. He had had a spiritual helper who would take over in the operations. (Perhaps such help is not uncommon. You may recall in Lisby Mayer's account in chapter 6 how a neurosurgeon would see light around patients as an indication of future success.) An extramarital relationship had brought problems for Frances's surgeon friend, and he had taken drugs to relieve the stress. He lost touch with the "Inner One" who had helped him with his surgeries, and a patient died as a result. In her garden, Frances and the surgeon did experiments with meditation and with Light transmission to her plants, the results of which they could observe immediately. Later, he was taken on at a higher level.

Frances frequently stressed the importance of Light, and recalled how she and Helen had worked with it on Earth. That was as nothing compared to the immersion of Light that she now felt. She described being in a great atmosphere of learning, as in a university, such as she had envisioned once when on Earth. There were outer courts and beautiful vistas of gardens where fountains of Light played. As she explored further, she found herself ascending the steps to a great open door. There the Light blinded her and she could go no further. She was back in her garden, struck by her inadequacy. Perhaps she would need another incarnation. She realized that she still had far to go.

We return to Frances's work in her rest home. The star patient was an eleven-year-old dancer named Jeannie, who Frances helped to recover from paralysis and reincarnate for a second try as an earthly ballerina. We hear how Jeannie is taken in hand by Frances, with the aid of Mother Florence.

Jeannie: I'll never be well; I've got a shrunken leg.

Frances: Not now, Jeannie. Your leg is quite well and strong.

Jeannie: I know it isn't. Where's my Mummy?

Frances: You can go and see her presently, when you've learned to run again.

Jeannie: Run? (Jeannie's attention was caught.)

Frances: Yes, run. We're going to teach you to run and play and dance here, Jeannie.

They worked together, tirelessly. In Frances's words, "[Jeannie] danced and whirled and twirled about as lightly as a butterfly. She ran from flowers to flowers; she skipped and sang and laughed for pure joy." Joy was what Jeannie needed. Soon she was ready to return to Earth again, to be a "real" dancer.

To show the darker themes, Frances is taken to the "Shadow Land," where more difficult cases are treated, sometimes for lengthy periods. There she meets a painter who lives in a little room off a dark street. On Earth he had been a promising artist, but he led a life of dissolution, on drugs and alcohol, and died in a brawl in which he killed another artist. Now he spends this solitary life painting ugly pictures in dark colors. In the background of each picture is a closed door. He can see no way out. Following much unproductive discussion, Mother Florence appears and the painter is given a palette of bright colors. Hope dawns. "He'll do! He'll do!" she declares.

Having given a description of her work as it then was, Frances goes on to talk about her experience of groups and the importance of the Group Soul and the different groups within that concept: family groups, special interest groups, and groups at higher levels. She ends with the message that life is a series of journeys on which she still has far to go, and she concludes that all is unity, and unity is Light.

In her predeath account, Frances tells how teaching was her main activity during twenty-five years in the High Anglican Community of the Resurrection of Our Lord in Grahamstown, South Africa, where she was principal during her last fifteen years. Alan Paton, author of *Cry, the Beloved Country,* met her in the 1940s and commented on her tremendous force of character and will power. An account of this period can be found in her *Frontiers of Revelation,* where she describes her early life and the religious experiences. Her book concludes with some thorough research into spiritual and mystical experience in a religious community.

Her time at Grahamstown ended with her decision to renounce her vows in favor of a less doctrinaire Christian practice. Frances's return to England led to a period of intense inquiry into spiritualism and many forms of psychic activity, during which she worked closely with Helen Greaves. *Testimony of Light* has been widely acknowledged as a book of deep wisdom.

A. D. Mattson's Experiences in the Afterlife

A. D. Mattson was a highly regarded Methodist minister and theologian who was also deeply interested in the paranormal, which he often discussed with his daughter, Ruth Mattson Taylor, saying that he would try to communicate with her after he died with an account of his experience.

Mattson managed to fulfill his promise. A year after his death in 1970, Ruth consulted her friend, the medium Margaret Flavell, and Mattson came through. They held many sessions, and Ruth wrote Witness from Beyond *and* Evidence from Beyond *describing these accounts, from which I shall quote instructive passages. What follows below are the main themes.*

- *When he arrived, Mattson had a close connection with family members who had passed before him and who gave him a great reception.*
- *On arrival, one starts on the astral plane, the level most similar to earthly conditions. Trained souls are there to work with new arrivals. One has a spirit body, suitable to the plane one inhabits. "One might think," says Mattson, "that at death we become clever, able to do anything we wish, with ease. Not so. We work at it. Children who die young also grow and develop, just as they would on earth."*
- *Mattson had been permitted to visit higher planes but could return to his astral body. "On earth," he tells us, "people may visit the astral plane in sleep. If they were to remember these experiences, it would be like living in two worlds—confusing. Such experiences are stored in the subconscious mind and are drawn upon during earth life."*

- *Mattson describes orientation classes in which he is taught various skills. Eight pupils sit in a horseshoe shape with a teacher. "We go into silence and direct our attention to the leader, who projects colors and collects sound, and redirects them toward us. Color is sound, sound is color." Each individual has a personal note, a sound used to attract their attention, when needed. "It is necessary to become very familiar with this returning to base," Mattson says, "for otherwise we would wander around, a lost soul."*

- *There are hospitals on the astral plane of the afterlife for the treatment of people who are not able to function effectively when they first pass over. The healers and physicians on the astral plane concentrate their treatments on making the patients realize that illness is only in their minds and that the mind is influencing the astral body, producing a simulated illness. Drug and alcohol addictions actually carry over from the earth body into the astral body. Withdrawal treatments must take place on the astral plane in these cases before wholeness can be achieved. It is far easier to break these habits while still in the physical body.*

- *Mattson describes lower astral states in the earth plane, which he says are a major problem. Some earthbound souls may remain there following accidental death or suicide. They may stay close to where they lived, as observed in some hauntings, or they may attach to others. Mattson is much concerned about earthbound souls and says that when they come from alcohol-or drug-addicted individuals, they may pose a threat to others during earth life by attaching to them and thereby attempting to satisfy their addiction through them. (I found this in my own psychiatric practice.) Mattson stresses the importance of prayer, both from Earth and beyond, in helping those who died by suicide or through violence. "It is important for all of us to remember that we should ask in all sincerity and then say, 'Thank you' and know that the prayer will be answered." As far as heaven and hell go, Mattson confirms that there is no Judgment Day. Heaven and hell are not places but spiritual states of being.[2]*

- *Reincarnation is paramount. In his daughter's book,* Evidence from Beyond, *Mattson describes in detail three incarnations that he experienced in different parts of the world. He gives much fascinating information on the subject.*

- *Mattson tells of afterlife contacts that he had with his brother, Karl, who was actively assisting highly developed souls who were leaving Earth. Mattson commented that his own main interest would be in helping those who were returning to Earth. He was not yet ready for this because he was unable to raise his vibrations to reach the top of the curve of souls traveling earthward. Instead, he had to catch them at the bottom of the curve, before they slipped in. As yet, he could only manage to make contact with those who were just beginning their descent, at about the second or third month of pregnancy. He hoped, eventually, to be able to work with souls for two or three years before they started their way down. To do that he would have to expand himself in consciousness and learn how to adjust his still somewhat earthly vibrations to the tentative vibrations of those souls. Mattson was much impressed by the schooling and instruction that the soul passes through before entering the black tunnel into the void returning to earth.*

- *Mattson tells Margaret, a medium, that her daughter was correct in saying that she thought you were going down a long, long while in a tunnel, and on waking, you're there and you cry because you've lost the comfort of the darkness of the tunnel and the close contact with the guardian angels who are bringing you down.*[3]

He leaves "you" for us to puzzle out. What amazing complex and committed activities!

The next chapter comes from accounts of the interlife obtained by Michael Newton through spiritual hypnosis, a technique that he developed especially for that purpose.

CHAPTER 11

Hypnotic Regression

Discovering Life between Lives

Michael Newton's approach to studying the interlife did not involve mediums. He did it himself, through hypnosis. This was not his first intention. His work as a counseling hypnotherapist developed in 1980 because of a client who was unusually talented in hypnosis. In trance, she went back into a previous earth life. Following that life, she went unexpectedly into an interlife before her current life. Newton called it "life between lives." Hypnosis had never gone this far before. Realizing that this was a great research opportunity, Newton spent the rest of his life exploring it. To do this, he had to develop his hypnotic technique to take clients to a much deeper level. This extended sessions to three hours, but the results made it worth the trouble.

He wrote books on his findings, and his approach became so popular that clients had to wait three or four years for an appointment. Accounts of two of these clients' sessions appear below. In reading them, you will learn how Newton's hypnotic approach (now practiced by many of his trainees) reveals a much more structured picture of the afterlife.

Classical Musicians Bring Fresh Pieces

Case 52 tells of an opera singer who experiences a wonderful freedom in the afterlife.

Dr. Newton: What is your major recreational activity in the spirit world?

S: To create music.

Dr. Newton: You mean with musical instruments?

S: Oh, there is always that—you can pull any instrument out of thin air and play it. But, for me, there is nothing more satisfying than creating a choir. The voice is the most beautiful of musical instruments.

Dr. Newton: Look, you don't have the vocal cords of an opera star any longer, so . . . ?

S: (laughs at me) Has it been that long since you were a spirit? No human body is needed. In fact, the sounds we create are lighter and of much greater range than those on Earth.

Dr. Newton: Can everyone sing the high and low notes?

S: (with enthusiasm) Of course they can. We all have the ability to be sopranos and baritones at the same time. My people can hit high and low notes and everyone is always on pitch—they just need a director.

Dr. Newton: Could you describe what you do?

S: (quietly, without boastfulness) I am a Musical Director of souls. A singing conductor—it is my passion—my skill—my pleasure to give to others.

Dr. Newton: Are you better at this than other souls because of your musical talent in your past life as an opera singer?

S: Oh, I suppose that one follows the other, but not everyone is as focused on music as I am. Some souls in musical groups may not be paying attention to the entire score. (smiles) Because of the musical range possessed by souls, they need a director to keep all these virtuosos on track. After all, this is recreation for them. They want to have fun as well as produce beautiful music.

Dr. Newton: So, you enjoy working with choirs rather than an orchestra?

S: Yes, but we mix it up to make the singing come together. When spirits apply themselves to instruments and voice sounds, it's wonderful. It's not stray notes. The harmonic meshing of musical energy reverberates throughout the spirit world with indescribable sounds.

Dr. Newton: Then all this is vastly different from working with a choir on Earth?

S: There are similarities, but here you have so much talent because every soul has the capability for perfection of musical sound. There is high motivation. Souls love this form of recreation, especially if they wanted to be able to sing on Earth but sounded like frogs.

Dr. Newton: Do you bring souls from groups other than your own to be in this heavenly choir?

S: Yes, but lots of groups like to sing opposite each other and see who can be the most innovative.

Dr. Newton: If you were to look into the deeper motivations for souls, can you help me understand why music is so important for them in the spirit world?

S: It takes you to new mental levels . . . moving your energy . . . communicating in unison with large numbers of other souls.

Dr. Newton: How large a choral group do you direct?

S: I am partial to small groups of around twenty, although there are hundreds of souls from many groups who are available for me to direct.

Dr. Newton: Large groups must be a great challenge for you?

S: (taking a deep breath) Their range is staggering . . . vibrations pouring out in many directions . . . everyone hitting incredibly high and low notes without warning while I am struggling with their cues . . . and yet it's all pure rapture.[1]

Graduation in the Afterlife

Case 54 is an individual who had personal problems in many incarnations, experienced over a period of one thousand years.

Dr. Newton: You seem very blissful about appearing in front of your council.

S: Yes, I have scrubbed off the last of my body armor.

Dr. Newton: Body armor?

S: Yes, my protective armor—to avoid being hurt. It took me centuries to learn to trust and be open with people inclined to hurt me as an outgrowth of their own anger. This was my last major hurdle.

Dr. Newton: Why was this so difficult for you?

S: I identified too much with my emotions rather than my spiritual strength. This created self-doubt in my relations with others whom I perceived to be stronger and more knowledgeable than myself—but they were not.

Dr. Newton: If this last major hurdle involved self-identity, how do you see yourself at present?

S: Finally, I used a rope of flowers to swing over the abyss of pain and hurt. I no longer give away too much of my energy unnecessarily. (pause) Physical and mental hardship has to do with self-definition. In the last 1,000 years, I have improved upon maintaining my identity in each life . . . under adverse circumstances, and to honor myself as a human being who could not be superseded by others. I no longer need body armor to achieve this.

Dr. Newton: What does your council say to you about your positive actions involving self-definition?

S: They are satisfied that I have passed this difficult test—that I did not let the adverse circumstances of these many lives dictate my vision of myself—who I really am. They are very pleased that I have reached a higher level of my potential through patience and diligence.

Dr. Newton: Why do you think you had to go through so much in your lives on Earth?

S: How can I teach others unless I have gone through fire myself to become strong?

Dr. Newton: Well . . . (subject interrupts me with something which has appeared in her mind as a result of my last question)

S: Oh . . . they have a surprise for me. Oh, I'm so HAPPY!

[At this moment my subject breaks down with tears of joy and anticipation of the scene unfolding in her mind. I pull out my trusty box of tissues and we continue.]

Dr. Newton: Move forward and tell me what the surprise is all about.

S: (bubbling) It's graduation time! We are gathering in the temple. Aru, my guide, is here along with the chairman of my council. Master teachers and students are assembling from everywhere.

Dr. Newton: Can you break this down a little for me? How many teachers and students do you see?

S: (hurriedly) Ah . . . some twelve teachers and . . . maybe forty students.

Dr. Newton: Are some of the students from your own primary group?

S: (pause) There are three of us. Students have been brought from other groups who are ready. I don't know most of them.

Dr. Newton: I notice some hesitation on your part. Where are the others of your own group?

S: (with regret) They are not yet ready.

Dr. Newton: What is the core color of all these students around you?

S: Bright, solid yellow. Oh, you have no idea how long it has taken us to arrive here.

Dr. Newton: Perhaps I do. Why don't you describe the proceedings for me?

S: (takes a deep breath) Everyone is in a festive mood, like a coming-out party. We all line up and float in . . . and I'm going to sit up front. Aru is smiling proudly at me. A few words are spoken by the masters who acknowledge how hard we have worked. Then our names are called.

Dr. Newton: Individually?

S: Yes . . . I hear my name, "Iri" . . . I float forward to receive a scroll with my name printed on the front.

Dr. Newton: What else do these scrolls have on them?

S: (modestly) It's rather private . . . about those achievements which took me the longest . . . and how I overcame them.

Dr. Newton: So, in a way, this is more than a diploma. It's a testimonial record of your work.

S: (softly) Yes.

Dr. Newton: Is everyone wearing cap and gowns?

S: (quickly) No! (then smiling) Oh . . . I see . . . you are teasing me.

Dr. Newton: Well, maybe a little. Tell me, Iri, what takes place after the ceremonies?

S: We gather around to talk about our new assignments, and I have the opportunity to meet with some of the souls who are in my specialty area. We will meet again in new classes that will make the best use of our abilities.

Dr. Newton: What will be your first assignment, Iri?

S: I will be nurturing the youngest souls. It's as if we will be raising flowers from the seedlings. You feed them with tenderness and understanding.

Dr. Newton: And where do you think these newer souls come from?

S: (pause) From the divine egg—the womb of creation—spun out like silken thread . . . and then taken to the nursery mothers . . . and then to us. It's very exciting. The responsibility will be so challenging.[2]

I have taken only two of the sixty cases described verbatim in Newton's book *Destiny of Souls*. All of the cases are given with great sensitivity and detail and are strongly recommended.

CHAPTER 12

Mediumship

Conversations with Spirits

Mediumship is the subject that, above all, we mostly associate with interlife inquiry in the Western world. Often it is seen as a direct way to the truth of what happens when we die. It is sometimes said that the most impressive cases are those in which the spirit of a deceased individual takes over the body of the medium and responds in the manner that was characteristic of his or her behavior when alive. This approach, although often satisfying for a family member wishing to make contact with the deceased, may provide little of interest for unrelated individuals.

However, there are notable exceptions, as in the case of A. D. Mattson, discussed earlier, who gave much highly evidential information and commented that his manner of speaking was uncharacteristic because he communicated by thought rather than words. Communicating through a medium is not an easy task. I have recently read the account of a communicant from beyond saying how a difficult job is made worse if the medium is not in good health or the sitters are suspicious and are asking critical questions.

Spirit rescue circle is a term often used to describe a mediumistic group that is performing the service of helping wandering spirits. "Spirit rescue" (by the group) and "drop-in communication" (by the spirit) are what happens. Since the presumed spirits are strangers to the group, there is no question of accidentally securing information through telepathy, which critics may suggest as an explanation when dealing with information that could be coming from deceased individuals who are known to group members. Intended communication with a known individual (Mattson, for instance) is directed, while drop-in communication is spontaneous.

Various techniques have been used for communication. Among these are automatic writing, the use of the Ouija board (not recommended for the curious, because it can be dangerous), mental mediumship (in which the medium receives messages through impressions, visions, and "heard" words), and trance mediumship (in which the medium goes into a trance and allows the spirit to take over the communication).

SPIRITS WITH THEIR OWN AGENDAS

Many times, in dreams, in spontaneous daytime appearances, or through mediums, we have messengers come to us from the spirit world with news of their own to impart. The case of Monsignor Robert Hugh Benson is an example.

Posthumous Author Keen to Have His Book Withdrawn

Benson was a Roman Catholic priest with interesting connections. The youngest son of Edward White Benson, Archbishop of Canterbury, Robert was ordained into the Anglican priesthood in 1901. He converted to Roman Catholicism in 1904. In 1911 he became privy chamberlain to Pope Pius X and managed the pope's household and appointments.

Benson was famous. He was known both as an authority on Roman Catholicism and as a novelist. His book The Necromancers, *for which he is renowned, was a romance in which a young woman helped free a man from demonic spirits. Benson himself had occult experiences that were frowned upon by his colleagues, who told him that he suffered from demonic influence. In* The Necromancers *Benson made his plot confirm the Church teaching, although this differed greatly from his personal experience. He felt guilty about this. Benson's death after a short illness, in 1914, seemed to end the matter from an earthly aspect but did not settle it for Benson in his continuing existence. He was determined to have his book changed or withdrawn.*

In 1951, Anthony Borgia, a clairaudient medium whom Benson had known as a boy, channeled a lengthy account, ostensibly from Benson, of his life since 1914. In it, Benson tells of his experience in "Summerland" and withdraws the statements made in his books. He also makes highly critical statements about Christian theology. To have made these statements while he lived would have meant a renunciation of orthodoxy and the loss of his reputation as a writer.

Benson gives a very full and detailed description of "Summerland" in which he includes an account of how he asked to have his views made known on Earth. He is told that this will be possible eventually. It happened in 1953, when his account was published as a book, *Life after Death in the Unseen Worlds.* I presume the delay was because Borgia first needed to develop his mediumistic abilities.

The spirit in our next account is perhaps less illustrious than Monsignor Benson, but his message is no less important to him and certainly provides some levity here. This account comes from *I Saw a Light and Came Here.*[1]

Thigh Bone Travels within Iceland

The Icelanders are a closely bound community, but even in Iceland communication can be a problem. At a séance held in Reykjavik in 1937, a drop-in communicator, when asked his name, replied, "What the hell does it matter to you what my name is?" One of the sitters asked the drop-in what he wanted. He was told, "I am looking for my leg. I want my leg." So began some years of tiresome labor.

Though appearing frequently to the group, the drop-in still refused to give his name. Only when another medium, Ludvik, joined the group in 1939 did things begin to move. The drop-in said that his leg had been built into the wall of Ludvik's house many years ago. Rude and difficult, the mystery man demanded coffee, alcohol, and snuff. Finally, Ludvik and another medium, Neils, issued an ultimatum. They would not talk to him until he gave his name. The man stopped coming, then finally brought news. His name was in the book in the church at Utskalar. At last, they had it.

Runolfur Runolfsson, nickname Runki. He died at age fifty-two, in October 1879, after getting drunk with friends and walking home along the beach alone. It was a windy night. Runki sat on a boulder and drank some more. He fell asleep; the rough sea took him. It was January when his body was washed ashore. Dogs and ravens had their fill. The remnants of the body were buried in Utskalar graveyard. Later a thigh bone was recovered from the beach and built into the wall of the house where Ludvik came to live.

In 1939 they opened Ludvik's wall and found the bone. Was it Runki's? The bone was long and Runki was six feet tall. His grave marking was lost, so they buried it in an unmarked plot in Utskalar graveyard. The village celebrated the bone's return. At a later séance Runki thanked them for the help and said he liked the party. He would be their spirit guide at later séances.

We're left to wonder, Why all the fuss? And now that Runki has that bone, what will he do with it?

Air chief marshal Sir Hugh (later Lord) Dowding (previously mentioned in chapter 10), the British commander in the successful Battle of Britain, included the two accounts below in his book *Lychgate*. Deeply troubled by his sense of responsibility for the deaths of 544 British pilots in the conflict, he began to use automatic writing to explore the evidence for survival of physical death.

Dead Munitions Worker Finds Sweetheart

Oh, how badly I want to write home and tell them it's all blather, this fuss about death. Can't you help me? I'm as much alive as I ever was. . . .

No, I'm not a soldier, only a munitions maker. I was done in in the last London raid. I was underground, and the floor gave way, and all the machinery on top came down onto us; it was an awful show, I screamed when I saw it coming. The fire broke out before anyone could stop it, and I saw it coming towards me—fire and tangled parts of machinery and molten metal; there wasn't a chance of escaping for any of us. The pain didn't last very long, but much longer than our bodies. I kept on feeling it whenever I looked at my body, and I couldn't leave it somehow until Jane came. Jane is a girl who worked near me; she came and took my arm and led me away.

Jane is a riddle; I knew it was Jane, but I'd never seen her really before, and suddenly I saw that she was LOVELY; her eyes and hair, and everything about her. I couldn't think why I hadn't been crazy about her all along, but she was just Jane to me, like a lot of others, dirty and tired and covered with oil-stained clothes. I said, 'Jane, but you're beautiful, and I love you,' and she just looked at me and laughed and said, 'Oh, Bill, ain't you soft. I've loved you always, but you had to be dead before you got some sense.'

'Dead,' I ses. 'Dead, wot the hell d'you mean? No, I'm not dead,' and then seeing I was getting all worked up, she soothed me like a child and told me not to worry. 'Well, I'm here, aren't I, Bill? And I aren't dead neither, so be a good boy and stop worrying.'

I did, and I followed her in a sort of sleepy way, I felt heavier and heavier until I slept good and proper, and when I woke up, I wasn't feeling nearly so strange and Jane was sitting on the grass nearby playing with two kiddies. I called to her and she brought them over to me. 'Look, Bill,' she ses, 'these are our kids.' 'Our kids,' I ses, 'not on your honour, I ain't got no kids by nobody,' and she laughs and ses, 'That's all over now, Bill, and I mean we've got to look after them . . . They was ours in some place long, long ago, least that's wot they told me; you see, Bill, we've lived through death, p'raps we've lived before we were born like, I don't know, but it don't seem as though we'd ever not been, if you can follow me. You and me, Bill, have got to scratch along together like, as we did on earth. But this is lovely, and we don't work any more.' I can't go on now. May I come again?[2]

Dead Soldier Finds Two-Year-Old Daughter Dying

He wasn't happy to be home with his unhappy family. He let them feel his angry thoughts until his deceased colonel told him that love was the only way.

"Murphy, there's more work that's worthwhile to be done, and your work too."

Murphy became aware of being called home by thoughts so insistent that he had to go.

It was wee Mary, our youngest, only two years old; and she got sick with the pneumonia, and the wife prayed and prayed, but it didn't do any good. I sat by her side, the wee one, she was so bad, I could feel her little hand all hot and feverish; and then suddenly she looked up and saw me, and climbed out of her cot into my arms, just like she used to do, and I held her for ever so long in great happiness. And then I thought maybe I'd best put her into her cot again, and as I went to do it, I saw she was in bed lying so quiet and still, and a child just like her was in my arms; and as I turned, uncertain what to do, a beautiful lady came and said to me, "Take her with you, no need to stay in the house now. Take her into the sunshine. She is yours now and for always, and she will be your special care."

So, I took her out and we sat on the hillside, and played with flowers and pebbles, and when I'd left her asleep out there, I went back into the house, I found only grief and mourning . . . and then I knew that wee Mary had come to join me . . . and I understood that death wasn't real, but Life everlasting was TRUE, TRUE, TRUE . . .³

In 1991, Michael Evans, a retired schoolteacher in Exeter, joined a rescue group of mediums and meditators to help the spirits of service men killed in the Gulf War of 1990, just as Dowding had done during the Second World War. The group had such success that they continued to meet when that task was over. The next account gives one of their cases.

In his booklet, *Billy Grows Up in Spirit: A Cockney Lad Returns after Death to Tell His Story,* Michael Evans presents the rescue group's sessions, in full, in twelve chapters. Some excerpts from these chapters are included below. There's quite a lot here, but I was charmed by it and thought you would be too. Every word of Billy's story can be read in the thirty-seven-page booklet, but it's currently out of print and scarce. Note that the speaker's names in the dialogue below have been added to the original version for clarity and ease of reading.

Billy Arrives

[First came two audible sniffs of the kind that one hears from little boys who have never known the use of a handkerchief. Then a lively cockney accent was heard.]

Billy: Allo!
Michael: Hello, what's your name?
Billy: Billy!
Michael: How old are you?
Billy: Me? Oh, I'm ten.
Michael: What happened to you, then?
Billy: Well, this bloke brought me along 'ere, you know, and then

this woman was talking to me just now, this one sitting here. She says I'm dead! Ha ha! I mean that's a laugh, in'it? I ain't dead, heh! Well, I don't think I am anyway.

Michael: Have you had an accident or anything?

Billy: Well, I was telling her just now, this lady that was here (he is speaking through her). Well, I can't tell you his name because it's not right, but my friend stole this car. He's a big one, he's bigger than me, and he says "jump in the back!" So I did. An' we went off in the car—I didn't think he could drive. An' we went whizzing down the road, you know. An' the bloody Fuzz (slang for police) was after us wasn't it!

So we drove down there an' all of a sudden there was a sort of a bang and I don't know what happened. I just got out of the car. I saw the Fuzz coming so I 'opped it. You know you're not going to stay there with the Fuzz round, are you?

Michael: Do you see anybody around you?

Billy: Well I got me friends over 'ere. I've made some friends. I told this lady, I don't know whether she told you or not, I went home to me Mum and I found me Mum crying. Tried to talk to 'er but she was crying so much that I just couldn't talk to 'er. I don't know what it was.

I thought, "Oh blow it! I'm going out!" Who's going to stay round the flats when you can go out, eh? So I went out.

I spoke to this bloke and he said, did I want to go and see Johnny? Well, he says, "He's in the hospital." I couldn't believe it. He says, "He's hurt, he's in hospital. Do you want to go and see him? We'll have to go on a bus," he says. So we got on this bus. 'Twas ever so funny though. We'd hardly got on it before we got off again. Heh! Funny sort of bus! And then, we didn't seem to ask no one, we just went in and there was Johnny, lying in bed. He didn't talk to me. I tried to talk to him but he didn't talk—I don't understand it. Seems funny, don't it?

Michael: Did they explain that you were dead and you're now in the next world?

Billy: No, they didn't say they was dead. They said they was just the same. We been living down under the arches, you know, that—what they call it—cardboard city. We live down there.

Michael: When you die, as you call it, you go into another world. It's still got people in it just the same.

Billy: When did I die, then?

Michael: When you crashed—when you crashed in the car. When Johnny got hurt. You see you got killed. That's why your Mummy's crying. She thinks you're dead, but you know you're not. She can't see you, you see, when you go back. You can see them, but they can't see you.

Billy: What about my mates that I met? Are they dead too?

Michael: That's right. They can talk to you.

Billy: Here, 'old on! That geezer's talking! He said he brought me here to try and understand and to listen to you.

Michael: Good!

Billy: It's like a bloody school, in' it?

Michael: No, not really. You don't have to sit in a classroom any more. You can just come and chat to us.

Billy: This bloke says he'll take me somewhere nice. He's a bit like a school teacher this bloke—but he's nice.

Michael: He'll look after you. Once you find what goes on, you'll have a whale of a time.

Billy: He says we can fly!

Michael: That's right!

Billy: Go on! (laughs disbelievingly)

Michael: Will you come back and tell us when you've flown?

Billy: Hold on! He says I'm to tell you I've been here a very long time. This is not recent.

Michael: Really! Can you remember what the date was when you were born?

Billy: (slowly) 1957, I think . . .

Michael: So when you were ten it was 1967. That's a long time ago.

Billy: I know I've been wandering round a very long time. Nobody's understood.

Michael: Well, you can always come here. We love to talk to you, and if we can help you, we will. If you will look about and ask if someone will help you, usually somebody comes. You've got to ask and you've got to look for the light.

Billy: Will they give me somink to eat? I'm hungry!

Michael: Yes! You can have something to eat. But you've got to ask first. Say, "Please can you help me?" Then you can have all the birthdays you've missed. But you must look for the light.

Billy's Education

Billy: You know me now, don't you? I've attached myself to you lot. I'm learning from you. That's why they let me come; it makes me think and start to learn. They say I can help you because I can help lift the vibrations. I don't know what they mean by that.

Michael: Well, it makes us feel happy. Have you made friends with some boys of your own age?

Billy: Yes. I went up on this lake and they showed us. This'll sound funny, but they didn't really do it, but it was like pretend fishing— like they do on earth, because you see we haven't done all the things you do on earth—but we didn't really catch any fish, they just showed us how people sit in the boats and do fishing. We didn't really catch any because the fish are too lovely to catch; they are beautiful, all pretty colours.

Michael: Were you able to touch them?

Billy: Yes, they came up and you could touch them. The teachers said we don't kill them, but they showed us the lines and we hung them over the side and they had a sort of bell on the end that made the fishes come instead of a hook. You can talk to the fishes. A funny tinkly sort of thought comes back. It's not like talking to you and me, you know. I can't quite explain it, but you get their thoughts and a sort of picture and a tinkly sort of feeling. They can send you their love, you know. It's lovely. If you swim, they can swim along with you.

Billy Brings Science to Earth

Michael: What are you up to now, Billy?

Billy: Nothing very new really, flitting around here, there, and everywhere. I've more or less finished most of the courses I was doing. I told you I was interested in the space thing and I've joined in a lot of that, you know. Cor, there's some things there, mate, I couldn't tell yer—you talk about science fiction, don't yer, but it's science fact to us. You see, you don't seem to realise it, well you do and you don't. You lot do, but other people don't—it's with us before it's with you. So, like when television was being invented, it was with us long before it was with you. We 'ad to get the idea back and we do that in several ways.

You might get somebody who is interested and we try and affect their minds to get the idea, but if that ain't possible then somebody 'as to come back and these are your famous scientists. You know them because they turn up in history—the ones that really do something—Who was that one? Logie Baird.

Michael: Yes, he was the television man.

Billy: You see, he couldn't get it back no-how, so in the end he had to take a life. Then what they do, they take a group of people, like I would be amongst them, and get it all ready and really work on each other's minds so that we could affect him more than someone who hadn't had that preparation. Am I saying the words right? When I'm over there I seem to be able to talk better. When I'm here I goes back into me cockney. I suppose you wouldn't know me if I didn't speak cockney.

We gets together like scientists do and we work out all the formulae. Then this one that wants to get it back, the main one of the group, we try and get that really, really into him and try and get it back with him but it doesn't always work so we have to come along and press buttons so that it comes through.

Somebody like him, like Einstein, like somebody that's alive now, poor soul, 'e's goin' through a lot but that's what 'e chose, and that's the man in the wheelchair—what's 'is name? Hawkin'? Yeah, you see, 'e's the same. 'E's someone what come back wantin' to get an idea through and the funny thing is that once 'e got 'ere 'e don't believe in us no more—ha ha—'e's goin' to get a shock when 'e come over, I tell you.[4]

That was a while back. Stephen Hawking's moved on. He may be with Billy now. I'm sure they'll get on famously.

The next account comes from Tricia Robertson's book, *Things You Can Do When You're Dead*. It tells how the financial director of a company, killed in a car crash, successfully passed on the information that a briefcase with valuable contents was hidden in the wreckage.

Robert Hartrick's Briefcase

Robert Hartrick came through as a drop-in communicator at a spirit rescue session, saying that there were important papers that could not be found. This meant nothing to the members of the rescue group. At about the same time, a member of the firm dreamed of Robert Hartrick on three consecutive nights. The first night he dreamed only that Hartrick wanted to tell him something. The second night he saw Hartrick holding up a briefcase in his left hand and pointing to it. This happened again on the third night, when he was also shown the image of a wrecked car, and a kind of zoom shot, looking deep down under the dashboard. This was associated with an impression of insistence to look in that place.

The next day, the dreamer went to the junkyard and, with the help of workers there, forced open the crushed metal under the dashboard and found a slim briefcase holding several important documents and a check for more than two thousand pounds, payable to the firm. It is interesting that Hartrick tried two methods to convey his message and persisted until it was received.

Robertson's book also has an account of multiple drop-ins acting over a period of months to communicate detailed information about the famous crash of the British airship R101, on October 5, 1930. It is an amazing story in which many of those who died came forward to tell of their concerns about safety before the flight. Keith Parsons tells the story on his YouTube channel.

The account that follows illustrates how a medium can provide more information about a situation involving a spirit's influence on the living. The information about mediumistic spirit release was given by Terence Palmer, who was active in the work and in training others. Terry's death from Covid, on December 31, 2021, was a great loss.

Dead Artist Finds Another Hand

The story begins in 1905 when Frederic L. Thompson, a goldsmith by trade, suddenly felt an urge to paint. Not since he was at school had he attempted painting, but now he was overcome with this strange impulse. Stranger still, he felt that it came from an American landscape artist, Robert Swain Gifford, whom he had twice met briefly, once to show him some jewelry, the second time outside, when Thompson was hunting. Gifford had died six months before Thompson had started painting. Thompson had the feeling that he was being taken over by the artist, and he often told his wife,

"Gifford wants to sketch."

Thompson was able to sell his Gifford-type art for good prices.
In 1906, Thompson went to an exhibition of Gifford's paintings, where he heard a voice say,

"You see what I have done? Can you not take up and finish my work?"

The matter troubled Thompson so much that in 1907 he went to see Professor James Hyslop, one of the founding members of the American Society for Psychical Research. Hyslop originally thought that Thompson was ill but then decided to take him to a medium, Mrs. Margaret Gaule, telling her that Thompson was "Mr. Smith" and nothing more. At once Mrs. Gaule saw an artist standing behind Thompson. She described Gifford's house and correctly said that it had to be reached by boat. She also spoke of a clump of trees with which Thompson had been obsessed for over a year and had painted.

Thompson visited Gifford's widow and was amazed to see on an easel a painting of the gnarled oak trees with which he had been fixated. Before going to see the widow, Thomson had left with Hyslop a drawing of the very trees that he now saw on Gifford's easel. Mrs. Gifford told him that her husband had often painted on the Elizabeth Islands. Thompson explored the islands and saw many of the scenes that he had been hallucinating. On his visit he heard a voice saying,

"Go and look on the other side of the tree."

There he found Gifford's initials, R. S. G., and the year 1902. Hyslop became fascinated by the case and took Thompson to two more mediums, who gave further confirmatory information.

Here we have a well-authenticated account, with much confirmatory evidence. What, I wonder, would have happened if Hyslop had followed his original thought that this was a psychiatric illness? This case differs considerably from the two patients described in chapter 3. They all had attached spirits, though only Thompson, the one who understood the situation, had no ill effects. However, I know that Terence

Palmer, a nonmedical therapist, routinely treated people suffering from attached spirits by working with a medium. In this way, harmful spirits are sometimes released within minutes and encouraging reports are often followed. Regrettably, essential follow-up research could not be done before Palmer's recent death.

Medium's Red Pajama Question

As young men, William James and James Hyslop, both of them professors-to-be in America, made the following agreement: The first of the two to die would send news to the other that death is not the end. William James, in 1910, was the first to go. Years later, when their youthful agreement was far from Hyslop's thoughts, he received a message from an unknown medium in Ireland. Did he remember red pajamas? This meant nothing to Hyslop until he recalled their time in Paris, years earlier. Their luggage was delayed and he went to buy pajamas. Red was the only color available. James teased Hyslop about this for days after. Unexpected by either of them, it was this red event that finally brought Hyslop to the state of accepting that survival really happens, pajamas or no pajamas. Hyslop was convinced by the message because when the medium had received it, she knew the name of neither man.[5]

The story is told in full by Colin Wilson in *After Life: Survival of the Soul*. In these cases, mediums helped shed light on the situation, but it was unnecessary for them to engage with the attached spirits, since they were beneficial.

CHAPTER 13

Liszt, Chopin, and Beethoven Instruct a Medium

New Pieces Played Publicly

The year was 1923. Rosemary is seven, alone in her bedroom, waiting for Mummy's call to breakfast and school. A strange man, with long white hair and a black gown appears. "I am a pianist and a composer. When you grow up, I'll bring music." The phantom fades. Would you have been afraid? Not Rosemary! This is part of her private world, her world and no-one else's.

Such scenes would continue throughout her life and bring many friends and interesting connections, even fame.

First is some background. In an old house in south London, seven-year-old Rosemary Dickeson lived with her parents and two siblings in a derelict house in a poor area. The father didn't work, though no one knew why. Where had once been a back garden stood a hall, which they rented out for meetings and ballet classes.

Rosemary wanted desperately to be a ballet dancer. To her dismay, her parents prohibited this, as they could not afford ballet classes. The spasmodic income barely sustained the family, and there was no money for more than necessities. Even so, from time to time, she managed to sneak into ballet classes, and she had sporadic piano lessons from three teachers. Her home piano had several nonfunctioning keys, so it was a relief to go to the teachers' homes. Practicing, especially in an unheated room at home, was difficult, and she often cried because her fingers were cold and stiff. Her parents had no religious belief, but they arranged for Rosemary to attend Sunday school. She was given a Bible, which she read from cover to cover with critical interest. Prayer became a part of her life, and she meditated and prayed deeply each day.

As a child, Rosemary was often ill. Rheumatic fever, acute anemia, and, in adult life, polio all affected her for long periods. Several times her life was "despaired of."

Rosemary didn't fit in with other girls. Her grammar school scholarship was happy but uncomfortable socially. Without the given school uniform, her poverty would have been obvious. She was modest but bright and inquiring. There was no further education. Office work was the best she could hope for. Rosemary married in her thirties and continued to live at the family home. Her journalist husband, a childless widower, was chronically ill, and they were so poor that, as her daughter later reminded her, they learned to enjoy potato dishes of every variety. Rosemary Brown (the married name, for which she was to become famous) suffered a double loss when in 1961 both her husband and mother died. She and the two children somehow survived on her earnings from helping in the school kitchen. Two years after the double bereavement, Rosemary broke her ribs from a fall. She had to stay at home. One day, sitting at the piano, she felt a new tune coming through her fingers. Liszt was back at last, with a group of fellow composers.

In 1963, her life's role took over. "Why me?" she asked. "Because you volunteered, in a previous life," said Liszt. He added that if she had acquired much skill on the piano, people might have believed that she had composed the music herself. Liszt introduced her to Frederic Chopin and other classical composers. The group taught Rosemary to present their new compositions to the world. Her life changed dramatically. Work came flooding in. First Liszt and then others guided her fingers, and all she did was practice, practice, practice.

She found Chopin exceptionally courteous and helpful with piano technique. In her book *Unfinished Symphonies,* she wrote the following.

Chopin, Her Favorite

We try it out on the piano. If I'm attempting a chord and my fingers are on the wrong notes, there will be a very gentle pushing and, if I let my finger be guided, it goes onto the right note. Then he says, all pleased, 'Ah, zat is right!'

Much of his new music is too difficult for me to play properly—I stumble through it, just getting some idea of how it should sound. For example, I was asked to play at the Albert Hall for the 1970 Remembrance Day service, and I asked Chopin if he would give me a new piece of music. It had to be very short as they were only giving me a few minutes.

'Mais oui!' he said immediately, and within a couple of days he had returned with a brilliant little study. Almost a little too brilliant, I thought. It took me weeks of practice to try and master the piece.[1]

Language could be a problem, but one day it proved invaluable. Suddenly Chopin stopped the music teaching and said, with agitation, "*Le bain va etre englouti!* The message didn't translate at once, but then the penny (or should I say the franc?) dropped." The bath, which Rosemary's teenage daughter had forgotten, was about to run over!

There was no shortage of willing composers. Chopin, Beethoven, Schubert, Bach, Brahms, and many more came to play, sing, or dictate new compositions. Rosemary used the old family piano. At the start she was scarcely a pianist. However, she was a determined, intelligent woman, and she worked with great commitment. At first Rosemary would allow her fingers to be guided, but later she learned to take down the music in writing. She became a frequent performer on radio and television, and her humility and honest endeavor won her many friends in England and abroad. While skeptics gave her a hard time, there were many supporters among musicians. Pianist John Lill, composer Richard

Rodney Bennett, and her biographer, Ian Parrott, gave her much public support.

It was not only the classical musicians who came to her. There were musical figures of more recent times. Here is Sir Henry Wood, founder of the London Symphony concerts, known as the Proms, speaking through Leslie Flint, a well-known direct-voice medium:

> "There are a crowd of souls, gathered together, most of us musicians, and we are all most interested in what is transpiring, and we are all working together in a body in the hope that we can make some impact on that world of yours and bring some reality and truth into it."[2]

The group seemed to see itself as a new-formed, unique organization, to bring a new spirit to Europe.

With the composers as neighbors, often demanding attention for new compositions, it was an extraordinary life. Rosemary alone could see the composers clearly in full detail. Communication presented difficulties as only some spoke English, and Rosemary's French did not always serve. Some, Liszt especially, became close friends. Liszt even accompanied her on shopping expeditions, drawing her attention, once, to cheaply priced beer. Liszt explained that finding her was no problem. He had only to think of her, and he was there.

Mind reading could be a problem. Since the composers were all adepts, they sometimes knew what she was thinking. One day, when Rosemary was practicing a piece with Liszt, who kept making her repeat it again and again, she had the thought, "Oh dear—he is a fusspot." Liszt suddenly disappeared. When he returned, three weeks later, he was very serious, and they began to work in a very cool atmosphere. They had been working for some time, and again Liszt was having her repeat a piece over and over when he suddenly stopped and said, somewhat quizzically: "I suppose I'm being a fusspot." The incident indicates how Liszt's habits persisted after death, and what a natural person Rosemary was.

In the following account Rosemary tells of a special meeting with Leonard Bernstein.

Rachmaninov Insists

There was a morning when I was terribly busy. I had all my shopping to do and I'd literally got my coat on to go out when Rachmaninov appeared, asking to finish a piece of music we had already been working on.

'Oh, I can't stop now,' I said. 'I simply haven't the time.'

He was very insistent, and persuaded me to sit down, and then said:

'It's important you take this composition. You will need it this evening, and I wish to give it a conclusion.'

He wouldn't tell me why I'd need his music and I wasn't sure whether or not to believe him. When the composers have a new piece to communicate, they are inclined to be rather demanding and not to be put off under any circumstances no matter how inconvenient.

Anyway, rather reluctantly I agreed to take the music down and fortunately we got it done quite quickly. Then he said good-bye, adding, with one of his rare smiles:

'Don't forget to take that with you tonight. It is important.'

He was quite correct. Later in the day, my agent, Barry Krost, sent me a telegram asking me to telephone him. I popped out to the phone-box around the corner, got through to Barry's office, and was told that Leonard Bernstein, the American composer, was in London, staying at the Savoy and would like me to have supper with him and his wife that evening at 11 o'clock.

'And,' Barry added, 'take some scores with you.'

Well, I was a little flustered by the whole idea. I felt that eleven o'clock was very late to be going out, and I didn't own the right clothes for visits to the Savoy or to meet people like the Bernsteins. I hummed and hawed on the telephone until Barry, deciding I was quite mad to hesitate to take the opportunity to meet one of the most famous composers in the world, said: 'Don't be silly. Of course, you must go. We'll send a car to pick you up about 10 30 p.m.'

Eleven o'clock that night found me arriving at the Savoy, clutching some of the composers' music, including Rachmaninov's piece. I was ushered into Mr. Bernstein's suite to find him taking a meal with his wife and my agent. Mr. Bernstein had been working very hard all the evening conducting, but he was full of life and welcomed me in a most friendly way. I was rather overawed, but he soon made me feel more at ease with his warmth and personality.

'Now, what will you have to drink?' he asked, 'Of course, you can have anything, but here in my suite we have only whisky and vodka.'

I had drunk neither previously, and hesitated, not sure what to say.

'Here try this,' he said suddenly, and thrust his own glass into my hand. I sipped the contents, wondering how many people had ever had the honour of drinking from the same glass as this great conductor. It was whisky, he informed me, and I found it rather strong in taste.

'Would you care for some chicken—it's very good,' Mr. Bernstein went on, 'or the shrimps here—they are simply delicious? Oh, I wish I hadn't thought of them. Now I want some!'

Presently he asked me what music had I brought, and I produced a number of scores from the brief case I had with me. He persuaded me to play, which I did with some trepidation, aware of my limitations of technique. Then he asked to have some scores to play himself. It became apparent that he is a marvellous pianist as well as a great conductor.

He liked very much the 'Fantaisie-Impromptu' in three movements which I had received from Chopin; in fact, he liked a great many of the pieces, Liszt's, Schubert's, Beethoven's, and the Rachmaninov's which, as the composer had predicted, interested him very much. It was a vivacious piece, very chromatic in nature—a real concert study—and Mr. Bernstein took to it greatly, and played it with great brilliance and remarkable speed, rolling out some of the passages like thunder. It sounded splendid, and I wished that I could make it sound as wonderful. There was only one piece he didn't seem to like: 'That's the only bar I don't buy,' were his exact words. But Rachmaninov has since embellished that, so perhaps he would 'buy' it now.

In the Chopin Fantaisie-Impromptu, there is a lovely theme at one point which caught the ear of both Mr. Bernstein and his wife. They had it played over several times as if they wanted to memorize it. I hope this item of Chopin's will be put on record eventually because it meant a great deal of hard work and patience on his part and mine, and has been hailed as a typically Chopin and very unified in structure.

I felt quite like Cinderella that night when I met Mr. Bernstein at the Savoy—especially recalling my days of menial labour in the school kitchens! He is such a charming and kindly man, and must be much loved as well as much admired; and his wife was equally charming and kind.[3]

In another passage, Rosemary tells a little about Debussy.

Debussy, the Artist

I find Debussy a very amusing sort of person. He likes to dress in what my daughter called kinky clothes, and he does appear to be flamboyant. Once he came in a sheepskin jacket with a straw hat perched on his head. He obviously enjoys wearing this sort of clothing, and it does rather suit him . . . He is quite serious in temperament. He hardly ever laughs and rarely smiles . . . Sometimes I think he is the most original of all the composers who work through me . . . Debussy is a very deep thinker . . . People who think deeply often are unorthodox . . . I suppose that, like Liszt, Debussy, too, was a victim of manners of his period.

Perhaps the most fascinating thing regarding Debussy is that he has started to paint now he is on the other side. And he has shown me his work. He'll just say: "I have a picture," and present it. He never asks whether or not I want to see what he has done, though, of course, he probably realizes how interested I am. The pictures are very beautiful and it is a great pity that the world can't see them. He is so proud of them himself, that I wish some way could be found for them to be shown.[4]

We must leave Debussy and move to Beethoven, who impressed Rosemary more than anyone. Here he is, in her words.

Beethoven, the Enigma

For a long time, Beethoven was an enigma to me. At first, he would communicate just by telepathy. He would impress the music on my mind without speaking a word. Although he would never name a note, I would just somehow know what he wanted to convey. I think perhaps the original communication might have been difficult and slow in coming because I was in terrific awe of him. At first in those silent meetings, I had a strong sense of his greatness; this real nobility of soul. The room was full of an atmosphere of sanctity. I was insufficiently at ease with him for much conversation to take place. But gradually I began to realize that Beethoven has, in fact, a great simplicity which is truly sublime. And having realized that, I became a little more confident in my attitude towards him. This perhaps encouraged him to begin to talk to me, and he began to speak in English, quite slowly, using short, easy words, and sentences in a very simple way, almost as if he were talking to a child—which I probably seem to be to him. Gradually a bond of sympathy began to spring up between us. I felt that though he was far above me, he did understand me. And I felt tremendously honoured that he would just stand there talking to me. Sometimes he talks about music, and sometimes he will talk about himself or life—or God. He says now he longs to pour forth great torrents of music which would really stir us into greater understanding; he wants to pour out his music for us in fountains of compassion. And he makes me feel that he aches to reach out to humanity and enfold us in wonderful love. He has an intense devotion to and belief in God with no narrowness in his thinking at all, and one day he was talking to me so gently and quietly that I felt very moved and very humble, and I said to him: 'Beethoven—I love you.' He just looked at me with the suspicion of a smile and said quite seriously: 'Of course.'[5]

Here's a bit from Rosemary's second autobiography, *Immortals at My Elbow:*

From childhood, I have led a prayerful life, always beginning and closing each day with spontaneous rather than formal prayer. I am a great believer in the efficiency of sincere prayer as a protection against undesirable spirits. It is interesting to note that music came to me from the composers at first only after I had been deep in prayer. Now, after several years of working with them, a brief period of inner prayer or silent meditation seems to suffice. I have carried out extensive and constant tests on my own mediumistic abilities, and also checked very carefully each composer or other spirit wishing to communicate. I still do this checking to this very day—much to Chopin's amusement, apparently. He came a few days ago to begin dictating a new piece of music to me—a Ballade, so he said. Suddenly he looked at me with a very solemn face, and said, in his broken English, 'Ah! I have forgotten to bring my identity-card. What shall I do?' That was so typical of his bantering manner that it was proof enough.[6]

Reading Rosemary's personal accounts has been a great pleasure for me. They are so fresh, interesting, and authentic. One cannot fail to warm to someone who writes, "I realize I am a musical nobody." How refreshing after the account in Wikipedia where not one of the strong professional supporters is listed, and one gets the impression that there is nothing whatever to be said in support of Rosemary's claim. In fact, she received much acclaim and recognition within musical circles. The pianist John Lill contributes a chapter to *Immortals at My Elbow,* in which he acknowledges the vocal support that he receives daily from Beethoven. Ian Parrott, an academic musician, in his book *The Music of Rosemary Brown* gives much technical commentary, including the following from Peter Dorling, the BBC TV announcer who produced "Mrs. Brown and the Great Composers" on BBC 1 on June 17, 1969. Dorling had been puzzled by the mechanics of the music's translation onto manuscript paper. He wrote:

> It certainly looks as if it is being taken down from dictation. I have watched the process many times and have often filmed it. You will know better than I do how normal composition actually happens: I had certainly never seen anything like the process Mrs. Brown uses. The music literally flows onto the paper in a continuous stream— sometimes both clefs together, sometimes one first and then the other. And all the time Mrs. Brown chats away: "Not so fast: did you say natural or flat? This G or the octave higher?" etc. and as fast as she can write, so it is taken down.

It is sometimes reported that famous composers have said that their compositions just come to them, without effort. Mozart said the tunes just walked into his head, unannounced, and Camille Saint-Saens said that in order to compose, he had only to listen. Rosemary was unique in many ways, but these comments indicate that her reception of compositions was not exclusive.

Rosemary Brown died in 2001. You can find her performing on YouTube. The scores of the music that she transmitted are in the British Library in London. Extracts from Rosemary Brown's *Unfinished Symphonies* have been included with the kind permission of her son Tom Brown.

CHAPTER 14

Hearing Voices

From Where? To Whom?

Thinking is difficult. That's why most people judge.
CARL G. JUNG (1875–1961)

Hearing voices is, of course, often equated with madness. That is far from precise and often wrong. "Auditory hallucinations" would be a more correct term for imaginary voices, but there is much more to this than language. Hallucinations are perceptions that lack the usual sense stimuli. They are not uncommon in healthy people and have often been experienced by outstanding individuals. The sort of things that might occur in mental illness are, for example, threatening snakes seen by a drunken individual or insults heard by only one individual when others (nonmediums) are present. It is easy to conclude that such hallucinations cannot be trusted and are best classed as rubbish. This is often so, but many hallucinated voices have real benefits. The philosopher Socrates heard an inner voice that warned him of impending trouble. On one occasion, while walking with his students in Athens, the voice warned him to turn back. He was just in time. Socrates and those who followed him escaped a herd of goats that came charging down the street.

Mahatma Gandhi, the religious and political leader, relied on an inner voice as his primary guidance throughout life. Joseph McMoneagle, decorated by the US government for his work as a remote viewer, writes how in the Vietnam War he frequently moved position suddenly, in response to an inner voice, and escaped death several times when minutes later the site he had left was attacked.

Without hallucinations there would be fewer, if any, world religions and the pages of history would contain fewer greats. And how about Rosemary Brown, whom we met in the previous chapter, and her flock of classical musicians whom she saw and heard daily?

Valid communication also occurs between living individuals at a distance, between incarnate and discarnate individuals, and between different personality parts. Hallucinations were high on the list of research priorities for the Society for Psychical Research when it was formed in 1882. At the time, scarcely anything was known about the causes of hallucinations, and it was commonly assumed that voices or visions, heard by one person only, were sure signs of mental illness. The "International Census of Waking Hallucinations in the Sane" (note the exclusion of the obviously ill) surveyed seventeen thousand people in England, Russia, and Brazil. It put the following question to them: "Have you ever, when believing yourself to be completely awake, had a vivid impression of seeing or being touched by a living being or inanimate object, or of hearing a voice, which impression, as far as you could discover, was not due to any external physical cause?"

The results of this ambitious research (nothing comparable has been attempted since) were published in 1886 in a vast two-volume book titled *Phantasms of the Living* by Edmund Gurney, Frederic Myers, and Frank Podmore. There were 1,684 positive responses. Of these, 493 participants had heard a voice. And it is the hearing of voices that we shall focus on here.

The following account from this book tells of an adventurous vicar who met a group of sailors and would have sailed with them, but he was discouraged from doing so by a voice.

Voice Saves Trusting Vicar

After meeting at an inn with a group of sailors, I agreed to join them the following morning to sail in their boat to a nearby island. I prepared for bed fully intending to go with the sailors but was unexpectedly interrupted as I was on my way upstairs to my room. I had got up about four or five stairs when someone or something said, *Don't go with those men.*

There was certainly no one on the stairs, and I stood still and said, 'Why not?'

The voice, which seemed as if some other person spoke audibly inside my chest (not to the ear), said in a low tone, but with commanding emphasis, *You are not to go.*

'But,' I said, 'I have promised to go.'

The answer came again, or rather I should say the warning, *You are not to go.*

'How can I help it?' I expostulated. 'They will call me up.'

Then most distinctly and emphatically, the same internal voice, which was no part of my own consciousness, said, *You must bolt your door.*

All this time I stood still on the staircase. . . . On reaching the room I lit a candle, and felt very queer, as if some supernatural presence was very near me. . . . At the very last moment (it was quite a toss-up which it should be), I bolted the door and got into bed. A great calm succeeded the past agitation, and I soon fell asleep.[1]

The vicar slept until late the next day and the sailors left without him. On entering the inn's dining room for breakfast, he learned that the boat he was to have sailed in had capsized and everybody had drowned. Where did the warning come from? The vicar said only that it came from within his chest.

INSPIRATIONAL HALLUCINATIONS

The "Census of Hallucinations" was limited to the sane and so avoided the hallucinations of the mentally ill, which form another important group. Leaving mental health problems aside for now, it seems likely that of all the thoughts, feelings, activities, and communications that enter conscious awareness, none have affected history so profoundly as inspiring voices and visions that have caused individuals to found religions and make other creative contributions to society. God is often suggested as a source of many inspiring hallucinations. Here are two of the many biblical references on which such beliefs are based.

When Jesus was baptized by John the Baptist, a voice declared, "This is my beloved Son, whom I am well pleased in!" (Matthew 3:17) This was heard by many others, an unusual feature of hallucinations. Hallucinations experienced by more than one person are not accepted by contemporary psychiatry (another example of science following theory rather than observation), because they do not fit the view that hallucinations must arise in the brain. For this reason, they tend to be dismissed as imaginary.

The Bible's most dramatic account of hallucination can be found in Acts 9:3–9 with the conversion of Saul (later Saint Paul), previously a persecutor of Christians.

Saul Hears Jesus

And as he journeyed, he came near Damascus; and suddenly there shined around him a light from heaven:

And he fell to the earth, and heard a voice saying unto him, "Saul, Saul, why persecutest thou me?"

And he said, "Who art thou, Lord?" And the Lord said, "I am Jesus whom thou persecutest: it is hard for thee to kick against the pricks."

And he trembling and astonished said: "Lord, what wilt thou have me to do?" And the Lord said unto him, "Arise, and go into the city, and it shall be told thee what thou must do."

> And the men which journeyed with him stood speechless, hearing a voice, but seeing no man.

It is notable that cases of mass hallucination such as these are rare. This adds conviction.

Within the religious and spiritual context, Moses, Jesus Christ, Mohammed, Emanuel Swedenborg, George Fox, Joseph Smith, and many more have heard voices ("revelations") or seen visions. Another highly regarded Christian figure, Saint Teresa of Ávila, wrote extensively about interior voices in her book *The Interior Castle*. Mohammed heard the Qur'an from the dictation of the archangel Gabriel, who declared, "Oh, Mohammed, of a verity thou art the prophet of God and I am his Angel Gabriel!"

Next we will learn how Roman Catholic priests heard from the dead.

I have never experienced instrumental transcommunication, but many people have, and they are really excited about its potential as another anomalous route to information that could illuminate the interlife. Undoubtedly another white crow. Instrumental transcommunication is about getting spoken messages from spirits through electronic recording apparatus of one kind or another. In his book *Is There an Afterlife?* David Fontana gives eighteen pages to this phenomenon. There is also the *Instrumental Trans-Communication Journal* online.

But where is our anecdote? No doubt there are many.

Spirits Use Technology

Dr. Fontana tells of two Roman Catholic priests who were investigating, in Milan University's Experimental Physics Laboratory, ways of filtering the taped sound of Gregorian chants in order to enhance their acoustic purity. A magnetic tape that broke easily exasperated Father Gemelli, who called, as was his practice, on his deceased father for help. On restarting the machine, the priests heard not the Gregorian chant but the voice of Father Gemelli's dad: "Of course I'll help you. I am always with you."

How astounding to have a Roman Catholic priest and his father's spirit in a demonstration (although unwitting) of instrumental transcommunication. The priests were so delighted that they requested an audience with Pope Pius XII, who thought the event might initiate a new scientific study for confirming faith in survival. What a forward-looking suggestion! Perhaps the pope saw the event as a gift from God. One wonders, might the incident give hope for combined religious-scientific research into anomalous events in the future? Such a combination is long overdue.

But the news isn't all good. Some years ago I heard from an individual who had become so impressed with instrumental transcommunication that he gave his time to it excessively. He subsequently heard abusive voices, which continued to trouble him. It is unwise to communicate with spirits in any situation without good reason and requesting protection from a trusted source. Christians might say the Lord's Prayer. Even such a competent medium as Rosemary Brown (see chapter 13) tells us she always prayed for protection before any attempt to contact one of her musical helpers, even though she knew them intimately. Negative interference is always possible. One cannot be too careful.

How amazing it is to have physical proof that the voices from the other world are real!

In addition to Socrates (mentioned earlier), many other famous figures from ancient times, including Pythagoras, are said to have hallucinated. So, too, did Joan of Arc, who, as an adolescent, led the French army to victories over the English. Her capacity as prophet and visionary is a large part of the story. Throughout her brief but brilliant military career she heard voices and had visions that guided her. These began when she was thirteen. At age seventeen, she was told to wear armor and lead the army. Her wounding and capture just over a year later were also foretold.

Of the many creative individuals outside the religious group who reported receiving inspiration from hallucinations, I name, here, only a tiny fraction: composer Robert Schumann, poets Milton and Blake, psychiatrists Carl Jung and Elizabeth Kübler-Ross, psychoanalyst Sigmund Freud, theologian Martin Luther, minister and activist Martin Luther King, and writer Robert Louis Stevenson.

Eileen Caddy, who founded, with her husband, Peter, the garden and community at Findhorn, Scotland, in the early 1960s, used to take down copious accounts of God speaking to her every day. In the early days this was mostly done, for hours, sitting in the lavatory (she doesn't say how the others managed!), because there was nowhere else she could be alone. Eileen and her husband believed absolutely that the voice was God, which it claimed to be. Certainly, the advice she received was of a high order and played a vital part in every decision they took in developing the community.

Here's a short piece from Eileen's autobiography, *Flight into Freedom and Beyond*. The event occurred a few years before they founded Findhorn.

A Voice Comforts Eileen Caddy

Eileen was living in a tiny cottage on the island of Mull, in a remote area in Scotland, with only her one-year-old baby for company, and a neighbor (the "simple friend" referred to below) who occasionally took pity on her and brought her necessities. One day, Eileen's isolation was eased by a comforting voice.

I was desperately lonely and there was such love in that voice, that my closed, angry heart began to soften. To begin with it was just a few words of love and comfort. I listened and more came, gently telling me to start to count my blessings. At first, I couldn't see any blessings. Then, as I looked around, I realised how blessed I was to have a roof over my head, a baby who was always so good and happy, and a simple friend who cared for me. I gave thanks for all the food, the fuel and the company. From then on everything became a blessing for me, no matter how small: a tiny patch of blue sky, a seagull on the window ledge, the postman delivering a letter from Peter. My whole outlook changed.[2]

PATHOLOGICAL HALLUCINATIONS

Before going further with this fascinating subject, we must ask, What does hallucination have to do with survival of physical death, the main focus of this book? Near-death experience, reincarnation, spirit attachment, and mediumship are closely connected to survival, but how about hallucinations? The answer is simple. Since hallucinations are common phenomena that cannot be explained by scientific physicalism, they are white crows of high significance, whatever their origin. They come under "indirect accounts," as described in the introduction. "Caw!" (I appreciate the corroboration!)

Doctors are taught to consider hallucinations to be sure signs of mental illness. Schizophrenia is not the only condition in which hearing voices is a characteristic symptom; bipolar disorder and dissociative identity disorder (multiple personality disorder) are other established conditions in which hallucinations feature.

I turn now to two psychologists and a psychiatrist for some examples.

Wilson Van Dusen, a psychologist in a Canadian psychiatric hospital in the 1960s and '70s, was fascinated by the hallucinations of psychiatric patients with chronic illness, many of whom had spent years, even decades, in the hospital. His interest began with a young woman who was distressed over her love affair with a man that she alone could see and hear. Van Dusen spoke to the hidden lover and asked the woman to repeat that man's words. He learned her story and was able to offer support.

He later developed a technique with many patients, and increased his understanding considerably. In some cases, he was even able to give the Rorschach inkblot test to both the patient and her hallucinated partner, as if they were separate people. Van Dusen said that these cases often resembled descriptions of spirit possession. From these he learned that the "voice" was often much less competent than the patient and that there are higher and lower orders of hallucinations. The following is one such example.

Feminine Aspect of the Divine

A voice that called herself An Emanation of the Feminine Aspect of the Divine was a great support to one male patient, a gas pipe fitter. In The Natural Depth in Man, *Van Dusen writes the following:*

I first sensed her gift in the form of all the universal symbols she produced. Some seemed to pertain to ancient myths. I went home and studied some obscure part of Greek myths and asked her about it the next time I saw the pipe-fitter. She had not only understood the myth; she saw into its human implications better than I did. When asked about the Greek alphabet, she playfully wrote the letters all over the place. The patient couldn't even recognise the letters, but he could copy hers for me. I remember once his turning in the doorway as he was leaving and asking me to give him a clue as to what she and I had just talked about. The Feminine Aspect of the Divine suggested the terms 'higher order' and 'lower order' to distinguish fundamentally different classes in the world of hallucinations. The lower order hallucinations were four times commoner than the higher order. The lower order had less talent than the patient, the higher order more. The lower order hallucinations lie, cheat, deceive, pretend, threaten etc. Dealing with them is like dealing with very mean drunks. They zero in on every fault or guilt of the patient and play on it. Their general aim seems to be to take over the patient and live through him as they please.[3]

Van Dusen's account of the "lower order" voices tells of the sort of experience that many patients have to tolerate, often for years, with little relief from psychoactive drugs. His patients disputed the term *hallucination*. For them the experience was intensely real. What is it like to experience negative "voices"? Here are two examples from John Nelson's book *Healing the Split*.

Voices That Threaten

Doctor: What have the voices been telling you recently?

Patient: They've been scaring me again. They keep saying they are going to take my children to their island and perform surgery on them, then make me eat their livers.

Doctor: Would you ask them where their island is located?

Patient: (after a pause) They said it's in purgatory.

Doctor: What name do they go by?

Patient: Friends of the Enemy.

Doctor: Please ask them if there is anything we can do to make them go away.

Patient: I've asked them that before. They just tell me to try swallowing poison.

Doctor: (frustrated) Ask them why they pick on someone like you, and why they don't just go back to their island and leave you alone.

Patient: OK . . . Uh, they said they like me because I'm so rich and sexy.[4]

Voices That Insult and Criticize

Another of Dr. Nelson's patients, Melissa, a fifty-four-year-old Mexican American woman, was distracted by voices for years, despite taking antipsychotic medicines. She regularly heard three voices, two males and one female, none of which resembled voices of people she knew in consensus reality. These unfriendly voices insulted and criticized her for the most ordinary actions. Once they spent days urging her to commit suicide, chorusing, "Do it, do it," until she took a small overdose of her medicines, after which they laughed and ridiculed her. Dr. Nelson continues: "When I asked Melissa to remember how her voices began, she recalled vividly that it was the day her husband died."

That night I saw him in my dreams and the next day I could hear him as if he were still at home somewhere. When I'd close my eyes, I could even see him. He helped me when I tried to figure out how to raise the kids and pay the bills, but sometimes he'd get mad and yell at me. For a while I had another boyfriend. My husband didn't mind at first, until my boyfriend started telling me how to raise the kids. Then my husband would argue with him, but of course only I knew what was going on.

One day I went to a curandero (medicine man) who my neighbour recommended. We never saw each other before, but when I walked into his room, he said to me right off, "Your husband has been dead for five years, but he's standing next to you right now."

I was so scared I thought I would pass out, because I knew he was right. He said that my husband loved me so much that he didn't go to heaven. Then he rubbed some holy water on me and prayed. I felt strange inside. Then he yelled and waved his arms in front of my chest, and I passed out for a minute. When I woke up, he told me my husband went to heaven. I never saw or heard my husband again, and I could finally sleep and rest.

About three weeks later, the voices I hear now began. They came when I was trying to fall asleep, and they kept calling my name. I think if my husband didn't go to heaven, he would have kept them away from me. I don't know. I tried to find the curandero again, but they said he went back to Mexico. The only thing that helps when the voices scare me is reading the Bible.[5]

Professor Marius Romme, the Dutch sociologist, found a way of helping voice hearers to help themselves. He appealed to the public. Romme's radio program in 1986 brought responses from 450 voice hearers. The subsequent conference, in which twenty voice hearers gave accounts of their experiences, led Romme to establish the Hearing Voices Network, a charity that is now active in about thirty countries. The work of the network is of great benefit to voice hearers, who have developed their own expertise to counter troublesome voices in ways that are rarely available through psychiatric services. They are told that, even though it may not be obvious, there is a reason for the voices, which relate to them in some way. Sometimes it is possible to bargain with the voices, perhaps by offering to listen only at certain times. Most helpful of all can be the mutual support that voice hearers gain from each other.

It is clear that hallucinations are meaningful and need our attention. Psychiatrists have too often taken them simply as evidence of psychosis and prescribed medication, which is often ineffective. Time taken to ask about the nature of the hallucinations is likely to be appreciated. Multiple personality disorder (a more widely understood term than the newer classification of dissociative identity disorder) needs also to be considered. Understanding has far more to offer than suppression. Not every case is due to illness. There is much still to learn.

CHAPTER 15

Seeing Apparitions

Visitations from the Dead

When my child falls in love, let me give thanks.
When my child finds that love can be for ever, let me
give thanks.
This branching tree will always be my home.
From deep in the canopy of leaves,
I will look down upon the birth of my great-great-great-
great grandchild.

WELSH PRAYER

When faced with circumstances involving extreme emotional or physical distress (especially when combined with prolonged isolation), some people have reported unexpected encounters with what they felt were helping, guiding, or reassuring spirits. One graphic account of such an experience was provided by Captain Joshua Slocum, the first man to sail around the world single-handedly, in 1898. Slocum endured conditions of extreme physical stress and profound isolation. In his account of this epic voyage, *Sailing Alone around the World,* he tells how at one especially difficult point on the journey across the Atlantic he became sick. (He had eaten too much fruit.)

Joshua Slocum's Phantom Pilot

Then I went below and threw myself upon the cabin floor in great pain. How long I lay there I could not tell, for I became delirious. When I came to, as I thought, from my swoon, I realized that the sloop was plunging into a heavy sea, and looking out of the companionway, to my amazement I saw a tall man at the helm. His rigid hand, grasping the spokes of the wheel, held them as in a vise. One may imagine my astonishment. His rig [nautical speech for clothing] was that of a foreign sailor, and the large red cap he wore was cockbilled over his left ear, and all was set off with shaggy black whiskers. He would have been taken for a pirate in any part of the world. While I gazed upon his threatening aspect I forgot the storm and wondered if he had come to cut my throat. This he seemed to divine. "Señor," said he, doffing his cap, "I have come to do you no harm . . . I am one of Columbus's crew. I am the pilot of the *Pinta* come to aid you. Lie quiet, señor captain," he added, "and I will guide your ship to-night."[1]

To his astonishment Captain Slocum discovered the next morning that his boat was still heading on the exact course he had put it on before he became sick and that it had covered ninety miles during the night through a rough sea. The phantom pilot reappeared in a dream the next night and said he would return whenever he was needed. Slocum says he woke refreshed, with the feeling that he had been in the presence of "a friend and a seaman of vast experience."

Another situation of prolonged social isolation occurred with Charles Lindbergh, the first man to fly the Atlantic solo. In his book *We,* he recounts the following story.

Charles Lindbergh's Transparent Companions

While I'm staring at the instruments, during an unearthly age of time, both conscious and asleep, the fuselage behind me becomes filled with ghostly presences—vaguely outlined forms, transparent, moving, riding weightless with me in the plane. I feel no surprise at their coming. . . . Without turning my head, I see them as clearly as though in my normal field of vision. . . . These phantoms speak with human voices . . . first one and then another, presses forward to my shoulder to speak above the engine's noise, and then draws back among the group behind. At times, voices come out of the air itself, clear, yet far away, travelling through distances that can't be measured by the scale of human miles; familiar voices, conversing and advising on my flight, discussing problems of my navigation, reassuring me, giving me messages of importance unattainable in ordinary life. There's no limit to my sight—my skull is one great eye, seeing everywhere at once . . . all-seeing, all-knowing.[2]

In this next account, a brother of a deeply loved sister, whose death from cholera in 1867, at only eighteen years old, had affected him deeply, sees her suddenly ten years later, when she appears briefly beside him, as if alive. He notes a scratch on her face that only their mother knew about.

Cheek-Mark Proves Survival after Death

This visitation so impressed me that I took the next train home, and in the presence of my parents and others I related what had occurred. My father was inclined to ridicule me, but he too was amazed when later on I told them of a bright red line or scratch on the right-hand side of my sister's face, which I distinctly had seen. When I mentioned this, my mother rose trembling to her feet and nearly fainted away, and as soon as she sufficiently recovered her self-possession, with tears streaming down her face, she exclaimed that I had indeed seen my sister, as no living mortal but herself was aware of that scratch, which she had accidentally made while doing some little act of kindness after my sister's death. She said she well remembered how pained she was to think she should have unintentionally marred the features of her dead daughter, and that unknown to all, how she had carefully obliterated all traces of the slight scratch with the aid of powder, etc., and that she had never mentioned it to a human being from that day to this. In proof, neither my father nor any of our family had detected it, and positively were unaware of the incident, yet I saw the scratch as bright as if just made. So strangely impressed was my mother, that even after she had retired to rest, she got up and dressed, came to me and told me she knew at least that I had seen my sister. A few weeks later my mother died, happy in her belief she would rejoin her favourite daughter in another world.[3]

The following account, first reported in the *Proceedings of the Society for Psychical Research*, came to notice through the "Census of Hallucinations" (1890) and is also found in Frederic Myers's *Human Personality and Its Survival of Bodily Death*. It is a case of a deceased relative appearing to a living one. In this case the apparition of Lucy Dodson's mother, who had died sixteen years earlier, had the important task of arranging the care of her deceased daughter's two children. Here is the account, as told by Miss Lucy Dodson.

Spirit Grandmother Looks after Her Family

June 5th 1887, a Sunday evening, awake between 11 and 12, my name is called three times. I answered twice, thinking it was my uncle, 'Come in Uncle George, I am awake,' but the third time I recognised the voice as that of my mother, who had been dead 16 years. I said, 'Mamma!' She then came around a screen near my bedside with two children in her arms, and placed them in my arms and put the bedclothes over them and said, 'Lucy promise me to take care of them, for their mother is just dead.' I said, 'Yes, Mamma.'

She repeated, "Promise me to take care of them.' I replied, 'Yes, I promise you;' and I added, 'Oh, Mamma, stay and speak to me, I am so wretched.' She replied, 'Not yet, my child.' Then she seemed to go around the screen again, and I remained, feeling the children still to be in my arms, and fell asleep. When I awoke there was nothing. Tuesday morning, June 7th, I received the news of my sister-in-law's death. She had given birth to a [second child] three weeks before, which I did not know till after her death. I had not known she was ill.[4]

It is interesting that the children appeared as apparitions in the arms of the grandmother, even though they were alive, elsewhere. Anomalous accounts are full of surprises. This chapter could have a hundred anecdotal accounts, each of them fascinatingly different.

Are they white crows? Certainly they are. That should not rule them out of consideration, of course. Why am I telling you this? Because in my view exploration of our inner world is of far greater importance than exploration of outer space. If we ask ourselves which form has the greater relevance for self-understanding and happiness, the answer will bound out exuberantly.

CHAPTER 16

Guiding Lights

Mysterious Orbs Lead the Way

Darkness cannot drive out darkness;
Only light can do that.
Hate cannot drive out hate;
Only love can do that.
MARTIN LUTHER KING, JR. (1929–1986)

In the book *Light Changes,* Annekatrin Puhle gives many accounts of people who benefited by a mysterious unexpected emission of light. The following is one such account and tells how she and her husband get caught in a sudden snowstorm while hiking up a mountain and cannot see which way to go to get down.

Blue Light Rescuer

We left our car in the village and began to climb [the mountain] at about 8 am in good clear weather. We have often climbed this mountain, and we both know it well.

As we were beginning our descent, at about 1:30 pm, the weather suddenly changed, and it began to snow hard. After half an hour, we had completely lost our way. The wind became stronger, the snow went on falling heavily, and we had no idea what to do. We were desperate.

Then, as we were walking along what we hoped to be the right direction back to the village, I suddenly felt a warm wind on the left side of my face. It was a strong wind, and it felt very pleasant. I turned my head to the left, and there, about five meters away, I saw a ball of light. It was a big blue ball about two meters in diameter, and it seemed that the warm wind was coming from it. I was very surprised, and frightened. I closed my eyes, but when I opened them again the ball was still here. I asked my husband if he could see it, but he said he could not. He plainly did not believe me and became very angry.

I took a few steps towards the ball of light, but it began to roll slowly away from me, just like a big snowball rolling on the ground. I felt attracted by it, as if hypnotized, and I thought that we had to follow it, although this meant that we had to make a right-angle turn away from our course. So, I told my husband that we should turn left, and although he still could not see the ball, he followed behind me.

We went on for about three hours, covering 15 kilometres, with the ball away in front of me, rolling along, and the same comforting warm wind blowing in my face. But then, very suddenly, both the wind and the light went away, and for a moment, I was absolutely terrified. But only for a moment, for I then looked around and saw the outline of a roof below us. I knew we were safe.

If we had gone on in our original direction, we would probably have had to go about 30 kilometres to the next village, and I think we would have collapsed from cold and exhaustion. Several people have been lost on that mountain.

I am quite convinced that the ball of light saved our lives.[1]

Here is another such account of psychic experience and research by Frances Banks (see chapter 10), author of *Frontiers of Revelation*.

A Softly Lit Path

Frances recalls how she and a friend lost their way at night in the South African countryside.

I remember looking up and trying to unite myself with the silent power of the heavens above. Presently I noticed a dim opalescent glow lighting my feet. Wondering whether it could be a last ray of the setting sun, I turned round, only to be assured that it had long since withdrawn all light. At the same time there stole over me a mysterious sense of, as it were, entering into another dimension—so difficult to describe, yet so characteristic of such encounters and so convincing. And now from my entire person, through the grey cotton habit I was wearing, there flowed this light I had never seen before—a soft, opalescent rose colour. Round our feet it made a circle, while for perhaps a score of yards ahead it etched the way of the cart-track as it wound up hill and down dale past the great bosses of palm-trees. We walked in silence, the light bathing us both and issuing in a steady, just sufficient, radiance . . . I can only say that no outer light has ever shone for me with such numinous effect as this light from within.

Napoleon Bonaparte claimed that he received military guidance from a dazzling star. He demonstrated this visionary capacity to one of his generals, as follows in the next account.

Napoleon's Guiding Star

In 1806 General Rapp, on his return from the siege of Danzig, having occasion to speak to the Emperor, entered his cabinet without being announced. He found him in such profound meditation that his entrance was not noticed. The general, seeing that he did not move, was afraid that he might be indisposed and purposely made a noise. Napoleon immediately turned around and seizing Rapp by the arm, pointed to the heavens, saying, 'Do you see that?' The general made no reply. Being interrogated a second time, he answered that he perceived nothing. 'What!' responded the emperor. 'You did not discover it? It is my star. It is immediately in front of you, most brilliant'; and becoming gradually more excited, he exclaimed, 'It has never abandoned me. I behold it on all great occasions; it commands me to advance, and that, to me, is a sure sign of success.'[2]

These stories are marked both by protective light and an unexpected savior. The white crow takes many forms.

CHAPTER 17

Telepathy in Humans and Their Pets

Long-Distance Connection and Communication

Distance means so little, when someone means so much.

Tom McNeal (1947–)

F W H M. What do these letters mean? Fire-eating Wilderness Hides Mosquitoes, Fastidious Waiter's Harmless Meringues, Frothing Water Holds Mouth-open, Freethinking World's Head-hopping Mystics? How about Frederic William Henry Myers?

Frederic William Henry Myers (1843–1901), classical scholar, poet, and founding member and leading researcher of the Society for Psychical Research, remains without doubt one of the greatest contributors to psychic research there has ever been. Myers's interests included the whole range of psychic phenomena, and his book *Human Personality and Its Survival of Bodily Death* is still regarded by many as the most authoritative book on the subject.

In 1882, Myers designed the famous cross-correspondence method for use in séance to establish proof of his existence after death. Those who would solve the messages required knowledge of Latin and Greek philosophy and history. May I leave it there? It is not something to be laughed at. A great deal of research has been attracted to the cross-correspondences, which are said to have given indisputable evidence of survival to those who have the time and energy to unravel the connections.

Myers was also the one to coin the term *telepathy*, or "distant feeling," which means the transfer of ideas and sensations from one mind to another without the use of ordinary senses. This autonomous communication is often facilitated by sleep, especially when one is dreaming. *The Afterlife Unveiled* by Stafford Betty has a fascinating chapter on Myers's account of the afterlife.

Sleep, especially when dreaming, facilitates telepathic communication. In the following account from his book, Myers reports an example of two-way communication between sisters who were sleeping a hundred miles apart.

Sister's Voice Calls in the Night

When I was a child at my home in Rochester, N.Y., my elder sister Jessie had almost entire care of me. In 1875 I was living in Fort Hartsuff, Nebraska, a military post, the station of my husband. My sister then lived, miles away, in Omaha.

One night in November I awoke from a dreamless sleep, wide awake, and yet, to my own consciousness, the little child of years ago, in my room in the old home; my sister had gone and I was alone in the darkness. I sat up in bed and called with all my voice, 'Jessie! Jessie!' This aroused my husband, who spoke to me.

I wrote to my sister the next day, telling her of the strange experience. In a few days I received a letter from her, dated the same as my letter, having passed mine on the way. In it she said that a strange thing had happened the night before: she had been awakened by my voice calling her name twice. She said the impression was so strong that she made her husband go to the door to see if it could possibly be I. No one else had called her; she had not been dreaming of me. She recognized my voice.[1]

While examples such as the previous account are interesting and worthy of study, telepathy research of a more standardized type comes in many forms. The first is "picture guessing," developed by F. W. H. Myers in 1890. In *Human Personality and Its Survival of Bodily Death,* Myers describes how one individual draws a simple, self-chosen, two-dimensional figure, such as a wine glass or a square. A percipient guesses and draws the same picture. In many such experiments the results are so closely related that the accuracy of the procedure is beyond doubt.

Picture guessing was improved upon by J. B. Rhine, who worked on it in the 1930s. Rhine was using Zener cards of five types, with specially gifted individuals and statistical calculation. One of the approaches he perfected involved individual "A" thinking about one of the five cards, and individual "B" guessing which of the five cards "A" was thinking about. Rhine's most remarkable results were published in his book *Extra-Sensory Perception* (1934). In it he gave the results of a particularly effective "guesser" (really a selector), a divinity student named Hubert E. Pierce, Jr., who completed 17,250 trials (twenty-five cards in each trial) of card guessing. Pierce guessed correctly, on average, twice as often as chance predicted. His results were statistically significant by many billions to one.

More recently, parapsychology researcher Rupert Sheldrake performed three different telepathy studies. One involved having four individuals send identical, unnamed, and unsigned emails to a fifth person, who, as each email came, had to guess the sender; another was similar to the first but involved telephone calls instead of emails; and a third was the study of dogs who knew their owners were coming home. In this last type, dogs would go to a window as soon as their owner decided to return home, although they were still far away.

The results in each group were strongly positive. The following is one such impressive case, first reported in Sheldrake's book *Dogs That Know When Their Owners Are Coming Home.*

Dog Finds His Way to a New Home

Tony, a mixed-breed dog, was left behind when his owners moved two hundred miles, from Aurora, Illinois, to East Lansing, Michigan. Six weeks later, Tony appeared in East Lansing and enthusiastically greeted his owner. Was there an objective clue to Tony's identity? Yes. While in Aurora, the owner had cut a notch in his collar.

While the notched collar gave clear evidence that it was the same dog who had worn the collar in Aurora, science would demand repetition. Where would we find twenty owners who would leave their dogs behind when moving a substantial distance?

Why is Sheldrake interested in animals, you may ask? Well, if humans can practice telepathy, why not animals, who probably depend on it? Our bodies and minds have many similarities. There are, in fact, many more stories that corroborate Tony's account—enough so that J. B. Rhine and his daughter, Sarah Feather, coined the term *psi trailing* to describe pets (dog, cat, or bird) who succeeded in tracing their owners who had moved far away from them, despite the fact that there was no possible sensory trail.

Many other cases can be found in Danah Zohar's *Through the Time Barrier.* Cats, Persians especially, turned out to be particularly gifted, or else managed to survive better without regular human care. One Persian, identified by a distinctive bone growth on the fourth vertebra of its tail, reached his vet owner three thousand miles away after several months.

Larry Dossey, author of *Healing Beyond the Body,* quotes another such amazing story recounted by Vida Adamoli in *The Dog That Drove Home.*

Pigeon Homes In On Hospital

A boy named Hugh Brady, who kept homing pigeons as pets, once found a wounded pigeon in the garden of his home. He nursed the bird back to health, ringed him with identity tag number 167, and kept him.

The following winter Hugh was suddenly taken ill and rushed to a hospital two hundred miles away, where he underwent an emergency operation. He was still recovering when, on a bitter snowy night, he heard a persistent tapping at the window. He called for the nurse and asked her to open it. When she did, a pigeon flew in and landed with a joyful flutter of wings on Hugh's chest. Hugh knew immediately that the visitor was his bird and a look at the number on its tag confirmed it.

Pigeons are famous for their homing instincts, but on this occasion the bird wasn't returning home; he had tracked his master down to a place he had no knowledge of and had never been to before. How he did it remains a mystery.

For me, the most amazing outcome was when I told an acquaintance who is a very active wild-bird feeder, expecting the same dramatic response that I had felt. I was sadly mistaken; she couldn't believe it. "No," she said, "that can't be true." I was saddened, almost in tears. But that is the story of this book, isn't it? Over and over, we humans are restricted by our own ideas.

The last area of telepathy research that I'll mention here, from an internet anecdote, involves Russian rabbits. Sounds a little cryptic perhaps, but bear with me.

Mother Rabbit's Telepathic Connection to Her Babies

Around 1956, Dr. Pavel Naumov conducted a research study on telepathy in rabbits. A female rabbit who had recently given birth was isolated from her eight babies, who were kept in a Soviet Navy submarine in order to assess whether communication, beyond the reach of electromagnetic rays, might be possible. The mother was at a laboratory ashore, with electrodes for EEG implanted in her brain. When the submarine was deeply submerged, many kilometers away,

assistants cut the throats of the babies, one by one. At each precise
moment of death, the anesthetized mother rabbit's brain produced
detectable and recordable reactions. When her last baby was killed,
the mother rabbit woke up and died.

The research is horrible, but since it gives information not available elsewhere, it is worth reporting. Science would again require its repetition, but I hope that such cruelty will never be repeated.

It is thought that the strong connection between pets and their owners remains even after one or both of them have died. The next chapter provides several accounts of animals reconnecting with their "former" owners from the afterlife.

CHAPTER 18

Animals in the Afterlife

The Loving Connection Continues

Until one has loved an animal, a part of one's soul remains unawakened.

ANATOLE FRANCE (1844–1924)

Pets await their masters in the afterlife, we're told. I've heard similar versions from two accounts. The first is from A. D. Mattson, whom we first met in chapter 10 and who, speaking from the afterlife, tells the medium that her friend Doff has taken the job of looking after dogs until their worldly owners arrive.

Animal Group Souls

Often, we have been on the astral plane during our sleep state with our beloved pets who have died, so the connection has been kept. But it seems that if we had pets in our earlier days and have no longer shown an interest in them, and have made no effort to seek them out, then these pets are enfolded and absorbed into the group soul of that category of animal. There is a dog group and a cat group and a separate group for all categories of animals, birds, insects, fish and so on. There the results of the experiences absorbed by every individual animal's core will be taken and added to the knowledge of the total group soul. In this way the level of intellect is enhanced, as are all instincts.[1]

Mattson's knowledge is strongly supported in *The Doorway,* an account recorded by Margaret Vivian through automatic writing. The chapter on animals very much confirms what Mattson says. Here is an excerpt that reminds us of earlier times. It must have been in the late nineteenth century.

Feeding Horses in the Afterlife

Many domestic animals would be entirely at a loss without man's company, and many soldiers killed in war spend much of their time in the animal sphere with their old equine friends. I know of one sergeant who at first went regularly to groom and feed his battery team, and it was some time before he understood that they no longer needed corn. I met him one day wandering about, looking for the forage store.

'What is it, Sergeant?' I asked, and he told that he could not find the stores for his team. 'They are in a nice field resting,' he said, 'and they have a shed to sleep in and a running stream, but horses cannot work without their corn.' So, I showed him where to get it, and for a time he fed the animals regularly. It was useless explaining that his horses would never have to pull the guns again, but gradually he came to realize that he and his team had shed their physical bodies.[2]

Cat-Drowsy

It seems that cats can create problems for their owners from the afterlife. For several months Joan, who worked as an airline stewardess, had been excessively sleepy, especially in the middle of the day, when she would experience an overwhelming urge to nap. It became so bad that she went to her doctor and asked to see me. This was an unusual referral for a psychiatrist, but Joan had seen me

*in connection with a troublesome phobia and thought I might be able
to help. I used hypnosis to learn what the cause might be and soon
found the answer, which almost woke Joan up. "It's Chouchou!" she
exclaimed. "He's with me!"*

*Her cat, Chouchou, had died six months before. During his final
months he had been excessively sleepy, so much so that he would
sometimes sleep all day. It seemed that after death, the sleepiness
transferred to his mistress. Being familiar with patients who were
troubled by the spirits of discarnate humans, I wondered, could
Joan's problem be the effect of a discarnate cat? Perhaps his effort
to stay with her was resulting in her sleepiness. I asked for a being
from the spirit world to take Chouchou. This worked. After that
my patient managed her job perfectly and never felt drowsy. How
about the future? If the sleep problem should ever follow the death
of another of her sleepy pets, Joan will know what to do. Provided,
of course, she can find a hypnotherapist to believe her. If not, she
will have to keep telling the cat to wake up, get out, and wait for
her on the other side!*

A sleepy house cat is bad enough, but how about big cats? Rosemary
Brown had a wealth of stories to tell us in chapter 13, but she didn't
stop at classical composers. In her third autobiography, *Look Beyond
Today,* she even features a tiger story. Here it is.

Tiger Remains on Guard

*Rosemary was sitting up with her asthmatic husband one night when
she became aware of an unusual animal smell. She felt a weight lying
across her. Slowly, that heavy weight became a shape with brown-
and-black stripes. She told her husband, who asked about the head
markings. That gave the answer. It was Sabrina, a tiger cub with
distinctive markings, which his family had reared in Egypt after
finding it distressed. Once domesticated, Sabrina had roamed the
grounds of their home as a nightly protector, an important role in*

their locality. And now Rosemary could see Sabrina, who had come to be with her old owner. She appeared several times, especially when they were about to leave their London home at night. It was as if Sabrina was saying, "Don't worry, I'm on guard." A useful character, but safer without her bodily abilities. There were also meetings with a cheetah, a bear that ambled off when blown at, and snakes that had belonged to a circus performer and seemed content to be ignored.³

Here's an amusing story. It comes from Ronald Russell's *The Journey of Robert Monroe*. Mark, a friend of Robert Monroe, whom we'll meet in chapter 20, was helping him develop a recording for one of his Hemi-Sync courses.

An Unfortunate Name

On entering the Park, a place in the afterlife where recently deceased people go, Mark became aware of his deceased grandfather. In the grassy field, Mark saw the grandfather's golden retriever, Winslow, running to greet him, with the grandfather coming behind. The dog remained after the grandfather had gone. Mark, imagining that this was an image from his own mind, asked if the dog had a message for him. The dog looked at him and said,

"Yes. When we meet next time, for God's sake, give me a better name than Winslow."

I mention this, not for investigators of survival and precognition, but for conscientious dog owners with a pet to name. You can shorten your list by one. Since the grandfather's death, the dog had been with his ex-wife. A couple of days after this, Mark heard that Winslow had been found dead in the woods. I don't know if animals take their names to Dog Heaven. I wonder what he is called today.

You may recall in chapter 1 that Dr. Nowotny's dog was confused at his master's sudden death and kept running back and forth between the body and the spirit figure, who was as confused as he was. Here's another account of dog awareness.

President Attends Own Funeral, to the Delight of His Dog

Keith Parsons, whose YouTube accounts of psychic experiences are so outstanding, tells of an account from the medium Geraldine Cummins, through whom President Franklin Roosevelt communicated in automatic writing. The ex-president told how he had attended his own funeral, where the only person to notice him was his dog, who rolled on the ground with delight at seeing his master. There is no record of how the president himself behaved on this solemn occasion. It may take a little while for presidents to get down to dog level.

From afterlife visitations from pets, we now move on to astral visitations from friends and family members.

CHAPTER 19

Astral Projection

Being in Two Places at Once

Traveling clairvoyance is also known as an out-of-body experience (OBE) or astral projection. Professor Charles Tart, a psychologist who has experimented and written on the subject, describes OBE as an altered state of consciousness in which the subject's mind is separated from their physical body. The self-awareness has a vivid and real sense to it, quite different from a dream. OBE is an aspect of nearly every near-death experience, but it may also occur spontaneously, without any dangerous situation to cause it, or it may be intentionally induced. It also occurs and is more commonly experienced in dreams, as we will see in the following accounts.

SPONTANEOUS ASTRAL VISITS TO LOVED ONES

These next two stories tell of people who unintentionally leave their bodies to visit friends and family members who are traveling great distances away. They are taken from the book *Human Personality and Its Survival of Bodily Death,* by Frederic William Henry Myers, founding member and leading researcher of the Society for Psychical Research.

Kissed across the Stormy Atlantic

Mr. S. R. Wilmot, a manufacturer of Bridgeport, Connecticut, sailed on October 3, 1863, from Liverpool to New York on the steamer City of Limerick, *of the Inman Line, with Captain Jones commanding. The night following a severe nine-day storm, he had the first refreshing sleep since leaving port.*

Towards morning I dreamed I saw my wife, whom I had left in the United States, come to the door of my state room, clad in her night-dress. At the door she seemed to discover that I was not the only occupant of the room, hesitated a little, then advanced to my side, stooped down and kissed me, and after gently caressing me for a few moments, quietly withdrew.

Upon waking, I was surprised to see my fellow-passenger, whose berth was above mine, but not directly over it—owing to the fact that our room was at the stern of the vessel—leaning upon his elbow, and looking fixedly at me. 'You're a pretty fellow,' he said, at length, 'to have a lady come and visit you in this way.' I pressed him for an explanation, which he at first declined to give, but at length related what he had seen while wide awake, lying in his berth. It exactly corresponded with my dream.

Mr. Wilmot's fellow passenger was William J. Tait, a fifty-year-old man who was not in the habit of practical joking. From the testimony of Mr. Wilmot's sister, Miss Eliza E. Wilmot, who was also on board the ship, he was impressed by what he had seen. She says:

In regards to my brother's strange experience on our homeward voyage in the *Limerick,* I remember Mr. Tait's asking me one morning (when assisting me to the breakfast table, for the cyclone was raging fearfully) if I had been in last night to see my brother; and my astonishment at the question, as he shared the same stateroom. At

my, 'No, why?' he said he saw some woman, in white, who went up
to my brother.

Miss Wilmot said her brother then told her of his dream.
Mr. Wilmot continues:

The day after landing I went by rail to Watertown, Conn., where my
children and my wife had been for some time, visiting her parents.
Almost her first question, when we were alone together was, 'Did
you receive a visit from me a week ago, Tuesday?' 'A visit from you?'
said I. 'We were more than a thousand miles at sea.' 'I know it,' she
replied, 'but it seemed to me that I visited you.' 'It would be impossible,' said I. 'Tell me what makes you think so.'

His wife then told him that on account of the severity of the
weather she had been extremely anxious about him. On the night
in question, she had lain awake for a long time thinking of him, and
about four o'clock in the morning it seemed to her that she went out
to seek him. Crossing the wide and stormy sea, she came at last to
a low black steamship, whose side she went up, and then descending
into the cabin, passed through it to the stern until she came to his
stateroom.

'Tell me,' she said, 'do they ever have staterooms like the one I saw,
where the upper berth extends further back than the under one? A
man was in the upper berth, looking right at me, and for a moment
I was afraid to go in, but I soon went up to the side of your berth,
bent down and kissed you, and embraced you, and then went away.'[1]

The descriptions given by Mrs. Wilmot of the steamship were correct in all particulars, though she had never seen it. Mrs. Wilmot states
that she thinks she told her mother the next morning about her dream,
"and I know that I had a very vivid sense all day of having visited my

husband; the impression was so strong that I felt unusually happy and refreshed, to my surprise."

A Night in Cairo

In the month of November 1864, Mrs. Elgee, on her way to join her husband, Major Elgee of the 23rd Royal Welsh Fusiliers in India, was detained overnight in Cairo. She had under her charge a young lady, who was going to India to join her parents. They were obliged to spend the night in a rather unfrequented hotel and were especially concerned as to their safety. Thus, they locked the door of their room, and then put a chair against it with a traveling bag so arranged on the chair that it would fall off if the door was pushed. As it was warm, they left open the only window in the room, for it led onto a small balcony, which was isolated and was three stories above the ground. Mrs. Elgee describes the events of the night:

I suddenly awoke from a sound sleep with the impression that somebody had called me, and, sitting up in bed, to my unbounded astonishment, by the clear light of the early dawn coming in through the large window before mentioned, I beheld the figure of an old and very valued friend whom I knew to be in England. He appeared as if most eager to speak to me, and I addressed him with, 'Good gracious! How did you come here?' So clear was the figure that I noted every detail of his dress, even to three onyx shirt-studs which he always wore. He seemed to come a step nearer to me, when he suddenly pointed across the room, and on my looking round, I saw Miss D. sitting up in her bed, gazing at the figure with every expression of terror. On looking back, my friend seemed to shake his head, and retreated step by step, slowly, till he seemed to sink through that portion of the door where the settee stood.

In the morning Mrs. Elgee determined not to say anything until Miss D. spoke about it.

Presently, on Miss D. waking up, she looked about the room, and, noticing the chair and bag, made some remark as to their not having been of much use. I said, 'What do you mean?' and she said, 'Why that man who was in the room this morning must have got in somehow.' She then proceeded to describe to me exactly what I myself had seen. . . .

Of course, I was under the impression my friend was dead. Such however was not the case; and I met him some four years later, when, without telling him anything about my experience in Cairo, I asked him in a joking way, could he remember what he was doing on a certain night in November 1864. 'Well,' he said, 'you require me to have good memory'; but, after a little reflection he replied, 'Why, this was the time I was so harassed with trying to decide for or against the appointment which was offered me, and I so much wished you could have been with me to talk the matter over. I sat over the fire quite late, trying to think what you would have advised me to do.' A little cross-questioning and comparing of dates brought out the curious fact that, allowing for the difference of time between England and Cairo, his meditations over the fire and my experience were simultaneous. Having told him the circumstances above narrated, I asked him had he been aware of any peculiar or unusual sensation. He said none, only that he had wanted to see me very much.

Mrs. Ramsay (who is referred to above as Miss D.) reports their conversation the morning after the incident as follows:

I believe I then told her it was not strange that I should look odd, for I 'had seen a ghost.' She started violently and asked me to tell her what I saw. I described it as best I could, and she said she had seen 'it' too, and that she knew it to be the form and face of a valued friend. She was much disturbed about it—as indeed so was I, for I had never indulged in 'hallucinations' and was not given to seeing visions.[2]

What do we make of these extraordinary accounts? They give impressive evidence of the intense connections that exist between certain individuals and occur, infrequently and unpredictably, at a distance. Their unpredictability makes them virtually impossible to study with the regular scientific method, which requires repetition. These phenomena give us yet more examples of the fascinating aspects of human behavior.

INTENTIONALLY INDUCED OBE

The following stories are of a much more exploratory nature as the individuals involved intentionally try to project astrally to loved ones who are some distance away. The first is an amusing case of a hypnotically induced OBE, described then as traveling clairvoyance, that took place in the 1850s.

Dog atop the Dinner Table

Mr Atkinson had mesmerised a young lady, the daughter of a medical man, who resided many miles from London, where the young lady was. She became clairvoyant, but her father, who came to see her, would not believe her. Mr A then requested him, when he got home, to do anything he chose, not telling anyone, at a certain hour and in a certain room. At the time appointed, Mr A mesmerised the young lady, and requested her to visit her father's dining room at dinner time. She did so and saw her father and the rest. But all at once she began laughing and said, 'What does my father mean? He has put a chair on the dinner-table and the dog on top of the chair!' Mr A sent by the first post an account of what his patient had seen, which was received next morning, and in answer he was informed that she had seen correctly, for that the father, to the amazement of the family, had put the chair on the table, and the dog on the chair, at the time agreed on.[3]

Thank you, Mr. Atkinson; thank you, young lady; thank you skeptical, ingenious dad, without whom we would have no story; thank you, compliant hound; thank you, curious readers who have inspired my writing.

The next story tells of three young people living in London long ago: a man by the name of S. H. Beard and two sisters, who were his close acquaintances.

Night Flights in 1881

S. H. Beard had been reading about the power of the mind. Was it really true that the mind could travel through space?

One Sunday night in November 1881 he decided to make the test. It could be simply done. At 1:00 a.m. he focused his thoughts on two sisters, who lived in a house three miles away. With his utmost strength he imagined a visit. It worked. The unbelievable happened! In calm exhilaration Beard wrote the following letter to Edmund Gurney, a seasoned researcher for the Society of Psychical Research:

On a certain Sunday evening in November 1881, having been reading of the great power which the human will is capable of exercising, I determined, with the whole force of my being, that I would be present in spirit in the front bedroom, on the second floor of a house situated at 22 Hogarth Road, Kensington, in which slept two ladies of my acquaintance, viz., Miss L.S.V. and Miss E.C.V., aged respectively 25 and 11 years. I was living at this time at 23 Kildare Gardens, a distance of about three miles from Hogarth Road, and I had not mentioned in any way my intention of trying this experiment to either of the above ladies, for the simple reason that it was only on retiring to rest upon this Sunday night that I made up my mind to do so. The time at which I determined I would be there was 1 o'clock in the morning, and I also had a strong intention of making my presence perceptible.

On the following Thursday I went to see the ladies in question, and in the course of conversation (without any allusion to the subject on my part) the elder one told me that on the previous Sunday night she had been much terrified by perceiving me standing by her bedside, and that she screamed when the apparition advanced towards her, and awoke her little sister, who saw me also.

I asked her if she was awake at the time, and she replied most decidedly in the affirmative, and upon my inquiring the time of the occurrence she replied, about 1 o'clock in the morning.

This lady, at my request, wrote down a statement of the event and signed it.

This was the first occasion upon which I tried an experiment of this kind, and its complete success startled me very much. Besides exercising my power of volition very strongly, I put forth an effort which I cannot find words to describe. I was conscious of a mysterious influence of some sort permeating in my body, and a distinct impression that I was exercising some force with which I had been hitherto unacquainted, but which I can now at certain times set in motion at will.

Gurney, a close collaborator of F. W. H. Myers, requested that Mr. Beard send him a note on the night that he intended to make his next experiment of the kind and received the following note by the first post on Monday, March 24, 1884:

Dear Mr. Gurney—

I am going to try the experiment tonight of making my presence perceptible at 44, Norland Square, at 12 P.M. I will let you know the result in a few days—

Yours very sincerely,

S. H. B.

Here is the account of the young lady Mr. Beard visited that night:

On Sunday night, March 22nd, 1884, at about midnight, I had a distinct impression that Mr. S.H.B. was present in my room, and I distinctly saw him whilst I was quite widely awake. He came towards me and stroked my hair. I voluntarily gave him this information, when he called to see me on Wednesday April 2nd, telling him the time and the circumstances of the apparition, without any suggestion on his part. The appearance in my room was most vivid, and quite unmistakable.

L. S. VERITY[4]

Here is another case of what is now termed "remote viewing." It too was stimulated by F. W. H. Myers's work. Myers remarks that the case has particular interest because it was reciprocal as well as being experimental. As we'll see, it is similar in these respects to the previous case.

Astral Visit from across the Corridor

One night in 1888, while in bed, reading, Miss Edith Maughan decided to reach her friend, Ethel Thompson, in the next room, by astral projection, about which she had read in Phantasms of the Living *by Edmund Gurney. She writes as follows:*

The candle was burning on a chair at the side of my bed, and I heard only the ticking clock as I 'willed' with all my might to appear to her. After a few minutes I felt dizzy and only half conscious. I don't know how long this state may have lasted, but I do remember emerging into a conscious state and thinking I had better leave off as the strain had exhausted me.[5]

The next day, her friend asked, spontaneously, if she had gone into her room during the night to frighten her. Myers remarks that the case has particular interest because it was reciprocal as well as being experimental.

ASTRAL ESPIONAGE

I wonder, could such things still happen? Today, in the twenty-first century, our lives are so different. We live in the age of electronic amusement in which we mostly receive rather than explore experiences. Besides, three individuals would scarcely be an acceptable research sample, and a proposal to enter a lady's bedroom in an out-of-body state and stroke her hair, without her permission, would surely never gain approval from a research committee. There are many more such cases to be found in the *Proceedings of the Society of Psychical Research* of that period. In those first years of the society, individual research and inquiry were of a quite different character to any other research before or since. Research methods need to adhere to the cultural norm.

Although these experiments with OBE and astral projection were light and entertaining, this discussion would not be complete without the mention of two more modern and serious aspects of remote viewing. This was developed for espionage by the United States, Russia, and China in the 1960s. The United States alone is said to have spent twenty million dollars on the project. Hal Puthoff and Joe McMoneagle, having worked for decades for the US government on the research and application of remote viewing, are in no doubt about the effectiveness of the project. McMoneagle was subsequently awarded the Legion of Merit by the US government in recognition of his achievements. Elizabeth Mayer gives impressive quotes from each of these authorities in *Extraordinary Knowing*. How does remote viewing confirmation equate with survival following physical death? It doesn't directly, but the white crows in this area are as free from darkness as white crows can be.

CHAPTER 20

Robert Monroe

Out-of-Body Explorer

Journeys bring power and love back into you.

RUMI (1207–1273)

Until I read Robert Monroe's books, OBE meant Order of the British Empire, as bestowed upon worthy subjects by the king or queen of England. Now I know better. Monroe didn't need a royal sovereign to honor him. He gave himself the initials. OBE stands for "out-of-body experience," the knack for leaving the body and going off for a bit of freedom elsewhere. People must have been doing this, privately, for millennia, but it was not generally known, except perhaps among shamans. Monroe found his own way, experiencing the fears and uncertainties of the unknown, and then reporting on how it was done and what he found. OBE is a complex experience that can vary from what Monroe reported, but we'll stay with Monroe for now.

I rank Monroe with other great explorers: Columbus, Scott of the Antarctic, Livingston, Darwin, the Curies. He is one of the top explorers of OBE, and he certainly deserves our close attention. Monroe's life was a combination of curiosity, enthusiasm, and commitment. He was an activist whose challenges he overcame, not principally by persuading others, but by taking them independently. In 1958, he embarked on his greatest adventure—the discovery of OBE. Monroe did not set out to make this discovery on purpose, however; it happened unintentionally, even unwillingly. In fact, he stumbled upon his inner world without even getting out of bed.

However, Monroe was no layabout. Ronald Russell's book, *The Journey of Robert Monroe,* is a feast of examples.

At four, Bob could read and write! After a week in kindergarten, he decided he must attend a proper school. His parents agreed, provided he could get there alone. To do so, he walked sixteen blocks and crossed a busy road (Bob's parents were different too!), clutching three cents for lunch, two cents for a peanut butter bun, and one cent for a cup of cocoa. At school, he developed a passion for music, and against his father's wishes, he learned the harmonica. Bob was a passionate person. He had passions for trains, fast cars (he learned to repair them when ten), airplanes, gliding, and sailing. He took control of a plane at the age of seventeen and got a commercial pilot's license soon afterward. Bob started college at fifteen. It was 1930, the year after the Wall Street crash, so it seems that rules were slacker than they are today. Many things were open to a daring teenager with a "yes" addiction. After flunking out of college, Bob spent a year as a hobo, an unsettled worker, riding free on freight trains. This was a seminal experience, as we shall see.

Bob was obsessed with women and although he narrowly missed marrying at age of seventeen, he was soon to marry, then marry again, and again, repeatedly. Between train trips, he was a salesman and learned to sell silk hosiery and tombstones (separately). Clearly his enthusiasm, his try-anything attitude, was unstoppable. He decided that college could be useful. College wasn't so sure. Bob persuaded them to take him back and changed from engineering to journalism. After graduation he went to New York, teamed up with three out-of-work actors, and wrote failed scripts for radio. The National Broadcasting Company noticed him. Soon he was writing and directing programs, each one with his personal stamp. To start with, Bob drew upon his hobo experience. *Rocky Gordon* was about the crew of a freight train, five days a week. It was a winner. He wrote the script, then went to the New York central railyard for the sounds of locomotives and railway stock. It was 1940. Radio was his love, but in 1945 he dipped into emerging TV, producing a daily theatrical piece for MGM, showing coming youngsters, with orchestra, for which he composed the music, not classical, but suitable. Bob's career blossomed, in what now seems a fairy-tale world. It was also a world of his making. He was devastated at being rejected for the war because of an eye defect, but he could turn anything his way. With a friend, he bought two planes and made thrice-weekly flights between Florida and New York. His friend died in an aerobatic display. Monroe sold the planes and supported the widow. He tried real estate, then went more fully into radio production, buying two radio stations to form his own company. Monroe saw radio as a more exciting medium than television. He experimented with sound to promote sleep and sleep learning. Money came and went. Three hundred thousand dollars a year, in the early 1960s, gave many opportunities, of which he made excellent use. This was only the hors d'oeuvre. The big change began in 1958. OBEs became his great adventure.

Nothing comes without preparation, however obscure. For a full year Monroe had curious dreams. He was flying, but above him were restricting wires that stopped him from flying high. Then the dreams stopped, but the movement continued. It started with whole-body vibration. Then he began to feel the sensation of rising out of his body. A few feet was more than enough. He struggled to return to his body. What if he couldn't get back? Desperately, he thought of bed. Imagination worked, and he made it back to his body! But what did it mean? Was he dying? Or losing his mind? A medical check showed that all was well.

He continued his experiments and soon got used to the experience. Fascination prevailed. He had to see what was beyond. Monroe continued his experiments with OBEs several times a week for years. He found his own way, experiencing the fears and uncertainties of the unknown and then reporting on how it was done and what he found. At first he remained in the neighborhood, checking on things he could later confirm, as in the following account.

A Pinch of Proof

While he was out of body, Monroe visited a woman friend on holiday, finding her with her niece in an unknown house. When he spoke to her, she seemed to respond, but he was not sure she would remember that he had been there, so he gave her a pinch. A few days later, she confirmed that she had been in that house at that time, but she had no recollection of the incident until he mentioned the pinch. Then she knew, and showed him a brown-and-blue bruise.

Such journeys were exciting at first, but they were to get a lot more interesting. Then came the biggest step; not a step, but a leap. On his OBE journeys, he saw people, mostly human, but not always, and they could change in new ways. Their bodies were not solid. One could walk through another person or a wall or a tree. There was no speech, as all communication was done by thought, and there were no secrets, because one's thinking was open to everyone else. In this world there were "parks" for people who had recently died. When Monroe told his friends about them, they asked him to find relatives there who had died recently. Sometimes he was successful, but he had to attempt it soon after they died, because they moved on rather quickly.

Monroe wrote a description of every session, meticulously. His book, *Journeys Out of the Body,* published in 1971, gave accounts based on 585 excursions. Sales took a while to develop but then generated fifteen thousand letters. These were mostly from OBE experiencers, expressing enormous relief to know that, after all the uncertainty, they were still sane.

Monroe was not only famous but wealthy and able to do as he liked. Without that freedom he could never have bought the estate and set up a facility called the Monroe Institute for the intensive and detailed research that he oversaw. The institute attracted specialists and interested individuals from all over the world and contributed much to Monroe's thinking. Monroe, explorer of the unconscious, followed its lead along the out-of-body trail. Curiosity and intuition provided the energy. Unlike other researchers, who read deeply about previous studies, he did his own thing. That came naturally because, as far as he knew, he was the first to explore this out-of-body world (different levels of the astral plane). There was no one to guide him. He also had the money to do as he liked, without having to apply to grant-giving bodies.

At the start, Monroe's interest in music and sound determined his focus on helping insomniacs and the further development of sleep learning. He was also interested in electroencephalography and studying the connection between conscious awareness and brain-wave frequency. One of his gifted visitors informed Monroe of observations, a century earlier, of music with slightly different frequencies for the left and right ears. Monroe saw the potential of this for inducing altered states of consciousness and developed the technique, later called Hemi-Sync (short for hemispheric synchronization), that became a regular method at the Monroe Institute for researching and inducing different levels of consciousness for individuals exploring their inner worlds.

Monroe thought deeply. He describes his ideas in his third and final book, *Ultimate Journey,* in which he uses the term *earth-life system* to name the conditions for life on Earth, where growth and existence, the need for nutrients, and reproduction are the predominant features. He uses the term *different overview* to describe the view he developed from his personal exploration of existence beyond Earth. In this he names the different states of consciousness reached with the use of Hemi-Sync, which can be learned in a six-day program available from the Monroe Institute. Monroe describes this as a step-by-step absorption of phase-shifting methods related to human consciousness. This is first used to release participants' fears and then to introduce them to other states of consciousness. The more notable of the different stages are numbered as follows: Focus 10, mind awake and alert, body asleep;

Focus 12, expanded awareness; Focus 23, a level inhabited by those who have recently lost physical awareness (died) but have not been able to adjust to this; Focus 27, the reception center or park, where those who have died are helped to adjust and move on.

Monroe died in 1994. The institute is now a nonprofit organization, with residential facilities and specially built rooms where people experience supervised Hemi-Sync awareness.

Ever-restless explorer, are you a meteor still?

In the next chapter we climb down from Monroevian heights and take a look over the shoulders of less exalted explorers.

CHAPTER 21

Dreams

Portals to Psychic Phenomena

A dream you dream alone is only a dream. A dream you dream together is reality.

YOKO ONO (1933–)

How can we visit anomalies in waking life and not look in on dreamland?

Dreams represent our inner landscape, where time and space and daytime "dos and don'ts" are on holiday. Most dream-people keep to their secret space and have the goodness not to disturb the sleeper, who upon waking, may have just the faintest knowledge that they were there at all. There are many ways of visiting and thinking of the dream state. Melinda Powell, author of *The Hidden Lives of Dreams,* puts it this way: "Dreams remind us that we belong to more than ourselves. They intimate that we are loved, not for what we know, possess, or do, but simply for who we are as children of a star-studded universe, alive with more-than-human consciousness."[1]

In ancient times shamans studied dreams for their wisdom. In the days before alarm clocks, television, and the internet, there was more time for such knowing. Living in a rush is not conducive to looking beneath the surface. Despite this, one message is clear: we sleep on the edge of the unknown, and our dreams have much to tell us. What that message is, however, is not always easy to decipher. The following are examples of my own dreams that fascinated me with their strangeness and variability.

Five Headless Bodies

This is one of the strangest dreams ever. There are five bodies: four small, one large, lying on the ground. They have no heads and no limbs, and they aren't moving. They are actually more like eggs than humans, and each has three lesser bodies within. The outer forms are children; the inner, grandchildren. All are Russian, and they are mine. However, there doesn't seem to be a connection to my family of five children and nine grandchildren, as none of us are Russian. Somehow, somewhere, within me, a system, totally beyond my understanding, is at work, and I have not the least idea what it's up to. Interesting!

The Picture Book

I am with an unknown child turning the pages of a picture book, the work of a friend. Pictures of people and country scenes are skillfully done in brown and green, all in the same style—impressive but somewhat boring. We admire them.

Planet Alongside

A vast planet, much like ours, has joined us, like a ship in the harbor. What an event! There is no panic. We only wonder what will come next.

Open Window

I am with my friend Peter, another psychiatrist, in a ground-floor room. He climbs out the window and walks along a path beside a road. I try to follow, but my legs cannot get through the open window. From the room the phone rings. I step down to answer it. No words, just deep breathing, like in a lucid-dream workshop that I had recently attended.

Blessed Walk

I'm walking along a deserted cobbled street in London. I am accompanied by a woman. We do not speak. I love the beauty of this cobbled street. At the end is a tiny drawer, which I know has something for me. I awaken. I feel blessed to be there. This dream came during the final week before sending my book to the publisher. I wonder if the street is my journey. Could the beautiful cobbles represent the stories, many of which come from long ago? Does the tiny drawer relate to this?

Do my dreams have meaning? The first two dreams stump me completely. The vast planet dream interests me: does it indicate the new spiritual connection that so many of us long for? The window dream could be saying something about career choices, though that is scarcely for this life. In "Blessed Walk" I am on a strange solitary journey. Could it be my book? Questions keep coming.

With such a wide variety of dreams, there have been countless attempts to classify them. Hans Holzer, in his book *The Psychic Side of Dreams,* describes several types of psychic dream. I list them here with my comments:

- **Prophetic:** Dreams that give predictions of events for which there is no possibility of action (see Mark Twain's account in chapter 22).
- **Warning:** Dreams that provide forewarning of an event that could be acted upon (see Eryl's dream in the Aberfan account in chapter 22).
- **Survival:** Dreams in which deceased individuals try to contact the living dreamer (see Robert Hartrick's account in chapter 12).
- **Reincarnation:** Dreams that tell of the dreamer's past life (see James Leininger in chapter 9).
- **Extrasensory perception:** Dreams that have psychic connections to actual events (see "The Find" in the introduction and the next two accounts given below).

- **Inspirational thoughts:** Dreams that contain new creative thoughts and ideas. The writer Robert Louis Stevenson describes his experience of being visited in dreams by brownies (see glossary) who would give him plots for his novels, such as *Treasure Island* and *Dr. Jekyll and Mr. Hyde.*
- **Nightmares:** Holzer's view on nightmares is that they are usually caused by physical problems concerned with illness or eating or drinking to excess. This was not my experience as a psychiatrist, as I found them to be particularly concerned with sexual or physical abuse.
- **Lucid:** Dreams in which the dreamer is aware that they are dreaming. With persistence and skill, it is possible to encourage and then manage the lucid state so as to make contact with the subconscious mind to help and heal the individual.

The following two accounts are examples of psychic dreams with connections to actual events.

Goodnight Embrace

In March, 1854, I was up at Oxford, keeping my last term, in lodgings. I was subject to violent neuralgic headaches, which always culminated in sleep. One evening, about 8 P.M., I had an unusually violent one; when it became unendurable, about 9 P.M., I went into my bedroom, and flung myself, without undressing, on the bed, and soon fell asleep.

I then had a singularly clear and vivid dream, all the incidents of which are still as clear to my memory as ever. I dreamed that I was stopping in with the family of the lady who subsequently became my wife. As I bid members of the family good night, I perceived that my fiancée was near the top of the staircase. I rushed upstairs, overtook her on the top step, and passed my two arms round her waist, under her arms, from behind.

On this I woke, and a clock in the house struck ten almost

immediately afterwards. So strong was the impression of the dream that I wrote a detailed account of it next morning to my fiancée.

Crossing my letter, not in answer to it, I received a letter from the lady in question: 'Were you thinking about me, very specially, last night, just about ten o'clock? For, as I was going upstairs to bed, I distinctly heard your footsteps on the stairs, and felt you put your arms round my waist.[2]

This next account comes from the 1886 book *Phantasms of the Living.*

Flight with Gravity

Somewhere about the year 1848 I went up from Oxford to stay a day or two with my brother, Acton Warburton. When I got to his chambers, I found a note on the table apologizing for his absence and saying that he had gone to a dance somewhere in the West End, and intended to be home soon after 1 o'clock. Instead of going to bed, I dozed in an armchair, but started up wide awake exactly at 1, ejaculating "By Jove! He's down!" and seeing him coming out of a drawing room into a brightly illuminated landing, catching his foot in the edge of the top stair, and falling headlong, just saving himself by his elbows and hands. (The house was one which I had never seen, nor did I know where it was.) Thinking very little of the matter, I fell a-doze again for half-an-hour and was awakened by my brother suddenly coming in and saying, 'Oh, there you are! I have just had as narrow an escape of breaking my neck as I ever had in my life. Coming out of the ball-room, I caught my foot, and tumbled full length down the stairs.

That is all. It may have been 'only a dream' but I always thought it must have been something more.

CANON W. WARBURTON[3]

The next account is by Maureen B. Roberts, Ph.D., a soul-centered psychiatric therapist in Australia. She tells of her shamanic work with Princess Diana, immediately following her violent death. Dr. Roberts's work impressed me greatly, in both details and sensitivity. I am grateful that I came upon it, as I feel it was written for all of us.

The Shaman and Princess Diana

On the night I heard about [Princess] Diana's death, I felt, as a shaman, an overwhelming desire to be of some help to her. The same night, I received far more than I'd bargained for in that I ended up spending the entire night with Diana in a long and complex Dream ritual. The Dream took place in what seemed like a kind of neutral ground, or in-between place; it was quiet and supremely functional—there were baths, pathways, and towels there—it was something like an ancient Greek garden, but with no sense of heaven; just a low-key, peaceful place for getting done what had to be done immediately there and then. It wasn't like any other place I've encountered in shamanic journeying, but featured lots of off-white stoneware and buildings, and other folk wandering about, absorbed in their own business. The Dream was also more feeling-dominated than visual, but the sense of personal reality was overwhelming and deeply moving. I could never do justice in words to the powerful feelings and images in this Dream; they were complex, reassuring, and distressing, yet overall, something very positive was, I feel, achieved.

Throughout this long Dreaming, I was very close to Diana and as part of a healing ritual, helped wash blood off her into a large white bath. I remember watching the blood swirl clockwise around and down the plug-hole, while at the same time we were talking in detail about the irreversibility of what had happened, and about the reality of the here and now. We'd also been talking about all this as we'd slowly made our way across the grounds to the bath. She found it hard to accept that she could not yet leave the place where we were, or that she was in fact dead; she was not overly distressed;

more like puzzled, tired, and regretful; but the main focus of the Dream was on her healing of soul and body, and on my offer— not in words, but simply as something that happened—to take on myself her woundedness. There was no particular point at which this happened, but suddenly I began to feel physically badly hurt, weak, and aching, as if I were recovering from a recent and devastatingly major operation. I looked down the front of my body, which was badly bruised from the upper chest area, and a huge, healing scar was running down my body. The scar was like a long clean scalpel cut—a thin line that was already closed up. I felt a kind of joy and wonderment at this, partly, I think, because—in a relieved fashion—I'd taken on the woundedness in a kind of recovery mode, without having endured the preliminary shock and horror of its infliction. I recall that this process—helping Diana wash herself free of blood, talking through what was now real, and feeling wounded—was enacted over and again in different ways several times, until there was an acceptance by her of death, after which I was free to leave her in peace.

I can't describe the kind of closeness this all involved; it wasn't what you'd call friendship, or sisterliness, or motherliness; it was (for want of better words) an indefinable sense of oneness, sorrow, patience, and compassion. For the next couple of days, I felt continual grief and profound emotion, and could not concentrate on any work, but I also felt at peace and immensely gratified (on her behalf and to the mediatory shamanic law of coinherence) that I'd been able to help out.[4]

Shamanism is the oldest spiritual activity known and must have existed for millennia. As currently practiced, it involves journeying to visionary Otherworlds. The law of coinherence just mentioned refers to the connections that shamans feel to the living universe at all levels. The dream of Princess Diana's passing has symbolic power for all of us. Is there anything more beautiful than helping another person in need?

• • •

Wilson Van Dusen, whose investigation of hallucinations was reported in chapter 14, was a psychologist of commendable curiosity. In his chapter on dreams in *The Natural Depth in Man*, he tells of some little-known research into the need for dreams. A study found that if sleepers were woken every time they entered REM (rapid eye movement) sleep, a cyclical state in which vivid dreaming occurs, and then were allowed to go back to sleep until they entered REM again, it upset them.

Van Dusen relates an experiment in which members of two groups of volunteers were studied. Group A members were awoken each time they entered REM, while group B members were allowed to continue sleeping. Both groups were allowed to sleep for the same length of time. After three days, Group A members became emotionally disturbed. After six days, they began to dream almost as soon as their eyes were closed, and they resisted being awoken. It seems that those deprived dreamers were not going to be interfered with any longer!

Recent research tells us that we dream throughout the sleep cycle, and that REM occurs only during story dreams. So it seems that REM dreams serve a particular need. "Curiouser and curiouser," as Alice remarked in Wonderland. Her remark fits perfectly in dreamland, too.

The dream world is a gift to welcome and explore. I wrote this chapter because dreams have much in common with other psychic phenomena. Since dreams are experienced by all of us, knowingly or unknowingly, I felt that I must include them, even if they usually defy our understanding. While not all of us are aware of psychic experiences, almost all of us are aware, at some deep level, of visiting our own mysterious dream world every night. That this is common, ordinary, and predictable is surely as remarkable an aspect of our being as anything else about us. It is an experience to be enjoyed, studied, and wondered about.

CHAPTER 22

Premonitions

Could They Have Prevented a Disaster?

Occasionally, some urgent message from the daily world makes its amazing presence felt, and we have a prophetic dream that declares itself by unusual vividness and is subsequently found to be true, as we'll see with the tragedy of Aberfan, a little Welsh mining town that made the world news in 1966.

Premonitions of the Aberfan Disaster

Ten-year-old Eryl Jones lived in Aberfan, and on October 20, 1966, she had a dream and tried hard to get her mother to listen to her:

Mummy, let me tell you about my dream last night. Mummy, you must listen! I dreamed I went to school and there was no school there. Something black had come down all over it.[1]

Mummy was too busy to listen closely. Anyway, it was only a dream. But it happened, as foreseen. The next morning at 9:15, the Pantglas Junior School was obliterated by a mass of coal sludge, estimated to weigh 150,000 tons, which slid down from the hill above. Eryl and 115 other children and their teachers died. Dr. John Barker, a psychiatrist and a member of the Society for Psychical

Research, visited the next day. He had a special interest in disaster prediction, and he contacted Peter Fairley, science correspondent for the Evening Standard, *who arranged for the paper to carry a notice on October 28, asking if anyone had a "genuine premonition" before the coal tip fell on Aberfan. There were seventy-six replies.*

Barker spoke to the most promising contacts. Here are three of them:

1. *On the day before the disaster, an eight-year-old boy drew a scene of many figures digging on the hillside, above which he wrote the words "The end of the world." The boy sensed something but failed to understand what it was.*

2. *Mrs. Grace Egleton from Kent gave this account: "I have never been to Wales nor do I have a television set. On the night of Friday, October 14th I had a vivid, horrible dream of a terrible disaster in a coalmining village. It was in a valley with a big building filled with young children. Mountains of coal and water were rushing down upon the valley, burying the building. The screams of those children were so vivid that I screamed myself. It all happened so quickly. Then everything went black."*

3. *Piano teacher Kathleen Middleton woke at 4:00 a.m. on the morning of the disaster choking and gasping, with a sense of walls caving in. She told her lodger about it at 8:00 a.m., which established the primacy of her experience.*

Whether these observations all came from dreams is unclear, but they all seem relevant for Aberfan. What can we learn from them? Eryl's dream was the only one that could possibly have been understood and acted on. Had the mother attempted to spread the alarm, she would almost certainly have been laughed at.

Emanuel Swedenborg—a towering genius, the Newton of the age, an engineer, metallurgist, mathematician, astronomer, philosopher, and theologian—began having visionary dreams at age fifty-five. Two years later, in 1743, he was seeing spiritual realms while awake. He stopped scientific work and wrote many books, of which *Divine Love and Wisdom, Heaven and Hell,* and *The Presence of Other Worlds* are still in print.

Swedenborg's psychic ability was well known. In 1760, Madame de Marteville sought his help with finding the receipt for a silver table service where the bill was being presented again. Swedenborg dreamed that Marteville's deceased husband told him that the receipt was in a secret drawer of a desk. This proved to be correct. The next year Queen Ulrika of Sweden decided to test Swedenborg by asking him to tell her the contents of a letter from her deceased brother. Swedenborg told her this in confidence. Later she said that it was a matter that no one else could have known.

Here is an account of Swedenborg's clairvoyance.

The Distant Blaze

In September 1759, at four o'clock on a Saturday afternoon, Swedenborg arrived in Gottenburg from England, and was invited by a friend to his house. Two hours later, he went out and then came back to inform the company that a dangerous fire had just broken out in Stockholm (which was more than 200 German miles from Gottenburg), and that it was spreading fast. He was restless and went out often. He said that the house of one of his friends, whom he named, was already in ashes, and that his own was in danger. At eight o'clock, after he had been out again, he declared that the fire was extinguished three doors from his house. This news occasioned great commotion throughout the whole city and was announced to the governor the same evening. On Sunday morning Swedenborg was summoned to the governor, who questioned him about the disaster. He described the fire precisely, how it had begun and in what manner it had ceased, and how long it had continued. On Monday evening a messenger arrived in Gottenburg, who had been dispatched by the Board of Trade during the time of the fire. In the letters brought by him, the fire was described precisely as stated by Swedenborg, and next morning the news was further confirmed by information brought to the Governor by the Royal Courier. As Swedenborg had said, the fire had been extinguished at eight o'clock.[2]

Swedenborg died naturally on March 29, 1772, having foretold the exact date months before.

As discussed in the previous chapter, many psychic experiences are linked to dreaming. The following prophetic dream was reported by Mark Twain, the American nineteenth-century writer, noted for his unusual and often humorous stories. There is nothing humorous about this account, which concerns the tragic death of Mark's brother, Henry, with whom he had been working on the *Pennsylvania,* a boat on the Missouri River, in 1858. Twain wrote in his diary, "I had a dream so vivid, so like reality, that it deceived me and I thought it was real."*

Mark Twain's Prophetic Dream

It occurred one night while the Pennsylvania *was laid up in St. Louis. Mark slept at his sister's house and dreamed that Henry was dead. "In the dream," he wrote, "I had seen Henry a corpse, as he lay in a metallic burial case on two chairs in the sitting room." Henry was dressed in a suit of Mark's. On his breast lay a great bouquet of flowers, mainly white roses, with a red rose in the center. Mark was so affected that he dressed and went to see where he assumed the casket was. The room was empty. He realized that he had been dreaming. Sadly, the dream turned out to be prophetic. A few weeks later, due to staffing problems, the brothers were separated. Henry was, as usual, on the* Pennsylvania, *but Mark followed two days later on the* Lacey. *When the* Lacey *touched in at Greenville, Mark heard a voice on the shore shouting, "The* Pennsylvania *is blown up just below Memphis, at Ship Island. One hundred and fifty lives lost."*

---

*At this time in his life, Samuel Clemens hadn't yet taken on the pseudonym "Mark Twain," but here I will refer to him by the name with which we are most familiar, "Mark Twain."

Four of the Pennsylvania's eight boilers had exploded. Henry was badly scalded and died from a misjudged dose of morphine. When Mark reached the Pennsylvania, Henry's body was in the dead-room. It was not in a simple wooden coffin, as was generally used, but in a metal coffin, bought by the women of Memphis, who had been impressed by Henry's special face and had raised sixty dollars. The diary records the following:

When I came back and entered the dead-room, Henry lay in that open case and he was dressed in a suit of my clothing. He had borrowed it without my knowing, during our last sojourn in St Louis, and I recognized instantly that my dream of several weeks before was here exactly reproduced, so far as these details went—and I think I missed one detail; but that one was immediately supplied, for just then an elderly lady entered the place with a large bouquet consisting mainly of white roses, and in the center of it was a red rose and she laid it on his breast.[3]

As we are learning from earlier accounts, it is not uncommon for dreams to foretell events. Despite the obvious contradiction of what our minds consider the commonsense notions of cause and effect, the theories of relativity and quantum physics accept the possibility of dream prediction. I profess no comprehension of these abstruse concepts, but am happy to accept that they agree with observations.

Many events, once thought to be impossible—powered flight, for instance—are now commonplace. Flight, of course, coming within the material domain, which was open to both observation and theory, could not long be denied. However, observations in the spiritual domain need a different approach, allied to the spiritual dimension, which is freed from space-time constraints. As yet, these are beyond our understanding. Even so, we can learn from observations, though the mechanism remains obscure.

CHAPTER 23

Heart Transplants

Memories of the Dead Live On

By tradition we think of the heart as one of the body's central points. It is formed from a unique type of branching muscle fiber and is closely connected to other body organs. Science regards it as a pump, a machine like the rest of us. Personally, I speak to my heart daily, breathing deeply, and I congratulate it on keeping me going. Even though it has been irregular for eighteen years and is far from robust, I fancy that we help each other as best we can. The Eastern view of the heart as the emotional center of the subtle energy system has my respect. In the West we regard the heart with reverence although we are unclear about its true depth and value. One example, the HeartMath Institute in California, which emphasizes bringing the physical, mental, and emotional systems into balance with the heart's intuitive guidance, is active and growing in influence.

It was William Harvey, the physician to King Charles I, who first described the nature of the heart's action and accurately described the circulation of the blood in humans in his book *An Anatomical Exercise Concerning the Motion of the Heart and Blood in Animals.* In 1628 he had good reason to fear that he would meet skepticism and abuse, and it took twenty years for his description to be accepted. Harvey's chief research tool was a small hand lens, which he used to examine animals from humans to snails. His methods were far from those of experimental research, but his thinking was clear.

Needless to say, basic heart knowledge has progressed vastly since then. Heart transplants, which would have been inconceivable in Harvey's time, are now almost commonplace, and they have led to some interesting psychological problems in a small proportion of recipients. These people report a sense of having the donor inside them, and they may experience a change in food and other preferences to match those of the donor. The recipient may also develop a previously unexperienced fear, as in the fear of drowning reported in the third account below. It has also been suggested that the soul of the donor may have transferred to the recipient. I am not aware of any research that has been done to clarify the cause of the psychological acquisitions. Certainly, the accounts support the belief that memory is *not* located purely in the brain.

Claire Sylvia's heart and lung transplant in 1988 was a great success. To her surgeon it may have been essentially a piece of expert plumbing. In *A Change of Heart,* Claire tells her story.

Claire Sylvia's Change of Heart

Claire, aged forty-eight, was a professional dancer, twice married and divorced. After the transplant she experienced things very differently. She felt rather than saw, and her feelings told her that the heart and lungs of an eighteen-year-old motorcyclist did not come unaccompanied. Her personality started to change in unexpected ways.

Being the first person in New England to have a heart transplant, Claire attracted much media attention. When, on the third day after the surgery, a reporter asked, "Now that you've had this miracle, what do you want more than anything else?" Claire shocked herself by saying,

Actually, I'm dying for a beer, right now!

She was mortified to have given such a flippant response. She had never even liked beer. But now, of all things, she was craving the taste of beer and feeling that only beer could quench her thirst. This was the first of many changes that Claire noticed during her convalescence. Other dietary preferences—green peppers, which before the operation she couldn't stand, and chicken nuggets, which she never ate—became essential. This made sense only later when she learned that chicken had been her donor's favorite food, and the nuggets were found in his pocket after the crash that took his life.

There were other changes, too. She felt more assertive, and she walked with a strut, as never before. She had dreams in which she was living with or getting married to a woman. Then came an unforgettable dream in which she was kissing a young man.

As we kiss, I inhale him into me. It's like the deepest breath I've ever taken.

And now she knows, without a word passing between them, that his name is Tim. Claire feels as if they will be together for ever.

There's much more to be found in Claire's book. Although the hospital wouldn't release details of the donor or his family, a friend of Claire's had a dream that identified the US state in which Tim had lived. Together, they found a newspaper photo that accompanied information about Tim's fatal accident. This led them to a meeting with his family.

Claire's book gave the first account of what it is like to receive not just the physical assistance of another's heart and lungs, but new feelings. What does it tell us? There's clarification from the next account, in which both donor and recipient are infants.

A New Heart for an Infant

The donor of this heart-and-lung transplant was Jerry, a boy of sixteen months; the recipient was Carter, a boy of seven months, with a congenital heart condition. Jerry's mother, a doctor, said that when five-year-old Carter first saw her, he ran to her and snuggled in, just as Jerry had done. Jerry's parents and Carter's parents first met at church. Jerry's dad, whom Carter had never met, was sitting in the middle of the congregation when Carter's family arrived. Carter let go of his mother's hand, ran straight to Jerry's dad, climbed on his lap, and said "Daddy." Such behavior, said Carter's mother, was completely out of character.

When Jerry's parents stayed the night at Carter's parents' house, Carter came to them in the middle of the night and cuddled in between them. Jerry's parents began to cry. Carter told them not to cry because Jerry said everything was okay.[1]

What is there to say about these transplant cases? Sylvia was well aware of the psychological changes within her. After the initial shock, she accepted them gladly. Later, she had a welcoming meeting with the donor's family. For the children, both donor and recipient seem to have accepted the change as natural and adapted well. Carter showed an awareness of the change and referred to Jerry as if he was actually within him; he was also able to recognize Jerry's parents.

These were amazing and welcome changes. A special awareness must have been transferred in both these cases. Was it the soul of the donor or some other knowing aspect? We cannot say. Reading these stories and those that follow, some of us may reach for the traditional grain of salt, whereas others may just accept them as conceivable.

In the next three accounts, we will see that the donor's mode of death caused problems for the recipient.

A Fear of Drowning

A three-year-old boy drowned in the family pool. His heart went to a boy of nine. Before the transplant, the recipient, whose home was on a lake, spent much time in the water. Afterward, he became very fearful of water but did not know why. He would talk to the donor, whom he felt was in his chest. The donor, he said, was very sad, saying that parents should look after their children. He had come from a broken home and drowned through neglect.

Dreams of Death

The donor, a policeman, was shot in the face as he made an arrest. A few weeks after the heart transplant, the recipient began to have dreams in which he would see the face of the suspected killer. A moment later came a flash of light, and his face felt very hot.

Paul Pearsall, in his book *The Heart's Code,* tells the following story.

A Memory Solves a Murder

An eight-year-old girl received the heart of a girl of ten, who was a murder victim, a fact that the recipient's parents did not know. When the recipient started having nightmares, she saw a psychiatrist, who learned the details of the donor's murder. These were reported to the police who were able to arrest the murderer.

While such cases have great interest, I doubt whether potential recipients are warned of possible psychological risk. It would be helpful for transplant surgeons to study these cases and cooperate with would-be researchers.

A final point: The cases of transferred memories after an organ transplant make it clear that the notion that all memories are held only in the brain is false. Such huge white crows cannot be ignored. Clearly, the heart is much more than a pump. "Caw, caw!"

CHAPTER 24
Energy Healing
Cures from Near and Far

Spiritual healing, also known as energy healing, has been a religious activity for millennia. Christians will be familiar with it from the King James Bible, which describes healing as one of Jesus Christ's main activities: "Thy faith hath made thee whole," he said to a man, who was then healed (Luke 17:19).

Healing was one of the chief activities of the Cathars, the Albigensian Christians in southern France who were exterminated by the Inquisition in the thirteenth century. Although it is no longer a specifically Christian activity, it is practiced by Spiritist followers of Allan Kardec and by many other groups and individuals worldwide. Spiritual healing challenges physicalism. It is one more example of an effective transfer of energy between individuals, outside everyday interaction— something foreign to physicalist belief.

When energy healing is done from a distance, it's known as remote healing. And when it is done without the recipient's knowledge, it is clearly more than a placebo effect (a treatment that works through psychological persuasion). Although much impressive research on remote healing has been done on animals, plants, and even unicellular organisms, physicalism can only say, "It cannot happen." This statement is simply untrue, and in this chapter we're out to demonstrate that it can and does happen.

The following account is an impressive story from a chiropractor named Sebastian, whose wife, Janet, died and now works with Sebastian as a healer on the Other Side. Sebastian tells Janet of a patient, and she and her team of spirits tackle the problem. In this case, the patients, Anne and her daughter, Mona, consulted Sebastian on the advice of a friend. Anne tells her story.

Baby's Insomnia Is Banished by Distant Healing

I am wanting to share my truly remarkable story and the intervention I have had from Sebastian and Janet, which has changed my life.

I am a professional working in the City of London and over 2 years ago, I got married and naturally decided to grow our family and have a child. Unfortunately, the first pregnancy resulted in a termination at 4 months. My husband and I were devastated but decided to move on and have another child. Mona had a normal birth. She was genetically normal.

The first 13 months of Mona's life were incredibly difficult. She would not sleep. As the months progressed, she woke more and more at night. Sometimes she woke 5/7 times. She always refused to sleep in my bed and she would never fall asleep if left alone in her room.

At 10 months we moved house and things got progressively worse with regards to Mona's sleeping. She lay awake for hours and would cry if I left her. I would spend hours getting Mona to sleep to then finally find her waking up after half an hour. I knew something was not right. We visited health visitors, several GPs and finally private paediatricians and they all fobbed me off saying there was nothing wrong with her. Mona suffered from gastric reflux and that was what I had thought was causing the problem. However, even medication did not work and this continued. I had even tried a sleep consultant who came to our house for a week and even she said she didn't know what was wrong with my baby and in her words, she felt like she had been 'hit by a train' the following morning!

I was getting very ill with the sleep deprivation. I had pretty much not slept since my baby was born and the attachment which she wanted from me alone was taking its toll. I was unable to focus, my eyes were blurry, I felt like I was having a breakdown. I was only able to take one day at a time and getting to the end of the day was my focus.

My friend Joan decided to visit me and, as she had driven far, asked if she could stay the night. The night progressed as it always did with me getting stressed and angry trying to put Mona to sleep, but she woke every hour. My relationship with my husband suffered as he was unable to support me or help with putting my daughter to sleep as she only wanted me. As a result, we were arguing too.

The morning came and Joan was shocked to hear the goings on of the night and was concerned. I broke down in tears declaring that I could no longer cope. I was desperate for help.

Joan got in touch with her friend Sebastian who I did not know. Sebastian told Joan that I had an 'entity' attached to me and that I had to see him urgently.

I spoke to Sebastian on the phone and he said if I was happy to accept, he would do distant healing. Now at this point I didn't know what he was going to do but I was open to any help that was offered. He asked me to be close and open and positive with Mona while feeding her.

From there on my life has changed forever. The next couple of days passed and I woke up one morning clear-headed, I didn't have a fog in my head (which at that point I thought was sleep deprivation), I could see out of my eyes; I felt happy and felt light and full of energy. I had no idea what had happened. I had also noted that that night my daughter slept!!

I phoned Sebastian to ask him what on earth has happened as I felt like my old self again which I had not felt for 2 years. He said there had been a spirit attached to myself and Mona. The spirit was sent to the light.

From there on and for the last few months I have been putting the pieces of my life together. What I have discovered is that with the first pregnancy that was terminated, the spirit was left behind and had decided to create revenge and wanted to split me and my daughter up. Sounds bonkers but very true. I was drinking milk all the time which apparently was the spirit controlling me. I hadn't driven for 2 years long distance as I had felt out of control. I had felt drained like the life force was being taken out of me, I was anxious and unable to feel happiness. My daughter suddenly was able to come to my bed and since then she sleeps with me. She wakes only once or twice and there is nothing unusual taking control of her.

Anyway, all is well now. However, it is a truly amazing story. Sebastian and Janet were able to help me and even though this is a field that I don't know anything about—it exists, it happened and distant healing worked. Thanks to Sebastian and Janet.[1]

This account came to me as I was writing this book. It fits perfectly with my knowledge of spirit attachment. Of course, one case proves nothing in general. But to Anne, little Mona's mother, and to Mona herself it is worth everything. Sebastian and Janet are happy too. I haven't come across such an account before, but I don't suppose it's unique.

Was Mona helped by healing or spirit release? I'll say that treatment was unconventional, and it worked. Most healers are happy to attribute success to Source, Spirit, or God. It's the effect that matters. If we can show that this case is another blow against unthinking physicalism, that in itself is good news.

But perhaps the next account will help physicalists bridge the distance to remote healing with a bit more ease. It details a more scientific approach, focusing on the mechanism of distant brain-to-brain influence. In November 2005, the *Journal of Alternative and Complementary Medicine* published a paper titled "Evidence for Correlations between Distant Intentionality and Brain Function in Recipients." The researchers worked in Hawaii, where there is a long tradition of healing.

Scientific Study of Remote Healing

Jeanne Achterberg and five colleagues persuaded eleven local healers who specialized in distant healing to participate. Each healer was to choose an individual Hawaiian with whom they felt a special connection. Each chosen recipient of healing was placed in an fMRI (functional magnetic resonance imaging) scanner for thirty-four minutes to record their brain responses. They were in an electromagnetically shielded control room, completely inaccessible to the healer. During this period, the healer was sending healing, by instruction, at randomly spaced two-minute intervals. The researchers were testing to see if the healing would show on the fMRI recording.

The results demonstrated that the Hawaiian healers, working remotely, were able to affect the blood flow in the brains of the recipients, as indicated by the fMRI brain recordings. The parts affected were the anterior and middle cingulate area and the precuneus and frontal areas. The findings were highly significant statistically.

This carefully conducted scientific experiment in a strictly controlled situation demonstrated very clearly that distant intention promotes clear changes in the blood supply and therefore in the activity of the brain's cortex in the intended recipient. This finding gives strong support to the view that one brain can affect another at a distance, even without a connection through ordinary perception. It doesn't explain how the effect is caused, but there is no doubt that it happens. The experiment gives impressive support to the scientifically minded, for whom observation rather than theory is of chief importance.

For the sake of accuracy, I'll just add here that "distant brain-to-brain influence" assumes that the healers' brains were the essential healing directors.

We now come to an account of healing in mice and humans that was highly effective.

◆ ◆ ◆

Dr. William Bengston is a sociologist who, for thirty-five years, has been active in healing breast cancer in both humans and animals. His method is known as Bengston Energy Healing Method.

Bengston learned healing when he was twenty, through his friendship with an older man who had developed clairvoyant abilities. For some years they worked together to develop a healing technique that was effective for humans. The technique enabled the minds of both healer and patient to be distracted from rational activities and included three treatment procedures: direct hands-on healing, transfer by a healing-treated cotton towel, and remote healing. It was effective for many conditions, especially those that had developed rapidly. Quick-growing cancer and Alzheimer's disease responded best of all. Cancer of the breast and many other areas could be cured in virtually every case. Injuries also responded well, but benign tumors and warts did not.

An important proviso was that treatment by radiotherapy or chemotherapy should not also be given to cancer patients. Those who received both healing and the routine medical treatments rarely survived. This could be because conventional treatments compromise the body's defense mechanisms. Bengston also insisted that any intending patient must first discuss the healing with his or her regular doctor.

Since Bengston is not medically qualified, his treatments cannot be termed medical, but medical or nonmedical, they work! He does not charge fees or seek custom.

Bengston also conducted a series of healing experiments using mice injected with cancer cells. The results were published in the *Journal of Scientific Exploration* and are so impressive that I set them out in detail here.[2]

Bengston Energy Healing Method

There were four similar experiments with hands-on healing. They consisted of the healer placing their hands on the cage containing five

or six mice, for an hour each day for about thirty days. The treated
mice achieved a cure rate of 86.9 percent, while the untreated mice
on the same site, none of whom were expected to survive, had an
amazing cure rate of 69.2 percent! It seems that the untreated mice
must have received remote healing unintentionally. The recovered mice
lived for the usual span of two years. There were also two groups of
untreated mice in a distant laboratory. None of them survived.

Before the experiments commenced, each healer underwent an
unusual training. It consisted of drawing up an ordered list of twenty
objects or objectives that they wanted in their lives. They had to work
through the list so as to develop a strong emotional attachment to
every item. The list had to be repeated faster and faster, so that the
items could be run through the mind in a matter of seconds. Only
then could they take on the healing. The final step was to insert an
additional item with an image of mouse healing.

Bengston supervised the training. I tried it myself (without
Bengston's help) and never reached the required stage. However, he
succeeded with six or more students. Something special must have
happened through the healers' preparation, since each of them subsequently became, like Bengston, left-handed, a strong indication that
the right brain activity was modified by the training process. Or possibly he was working through them, and hence not working through
me. Bengston makes the point that all the trained healers were skeptical (there were no members of the Skeptics Society though!), and
none of them had expressed any "faith" in the outcome. The fact that
Bengston was able, with this method, to train effective new healers is
plainly an important step.

I have been particularly impressed by Bengston's work. His active
research continues, and I hope that when medical doctors finally turn
to noninvasive treatments for cancer, Bengston's contribution through
his work on both mice and humans will be fully acknowledged and he
will receive the support he deserves.

Isn't healing exciting? I've learned a lot. Clearly there is much more to learn. One thing is certain: when you began reading this chapter, you were not expecting stories anything like these. Or were you? Perhaps you were. I hear a comment. Did you hear that, readers? Now it's even louder. "Caw! Caw!"

CHAPTER 25

Last Thoughts

The decisive question for man is: Is he related to something
infinite or not? That is the telling question of his life.

CARL G. JUNG (1875–1961)

We're at the end of what has been a very important choice for me. I have chosen to write a book on the most momentous subject I know: survival of physical death. My book is primarily for the general public, especially those who are by nature questioners. To any psychiatrist who has traveled with us, I hope you have felt stimulated. I was exposed to the truth in my work as a psychiatrist. Naturally I wish to pass it on. For every reader I have three messages:

1. We survive bodily death. It is the truth of truths, so far as our lives on the planet are concerned.
2. Contemporary science, as believed and practiced today, is highly misleading and is taking us astray.
3. Anomalous experience indicates the presence of the mystical reality that surrounds us.

Here you have read of scores of accounts about psychic experiences. They are of great importance because they challenge the physicalist claim that existence is a chance event and that our lives are meaning-less. Since so many people accept this false claim as truth, they feel lost in our chaotic thought-world of denial. The great truth for all of us is this: bodily death is not the end; it is simply a transition to something immensely wider and greater.

Dying gives meaning to life. Life decisions are growth decisions. Each step takes us farther, within this life and beyond. Karma, the ancient yet growing influence that one's behavior in this life has on later lives, is believed by many to play a major part in determining our future. In this way, belief in karma affects both individual and group behavior and is a vital force in shaping our society.

We live at a crucial time. The future of Earth depends on our behavior. We must develop a positive, nonexploitative relationship with the living world we share. The ecological crisis that has overtaken our planet has grown directly through industrial capitalism, fathered by the philosophy of physicality, which denies the spiritual nature of life and has led to the excessive exploitation of world resources. The COVID pandemic, in turn, has brought an increasing awareness of the irrele-vance of national boundaries. More and more we are coming to accept that we share common problems and common aims. It is also making us more aware of the colossal break that now separates humanity from its formative relationship with nature. We live behind walls, and the walls keep us from each other and from everything that is fresh and alive.

I have an unusual authority, the result of a most unusual experi-ence. As a psychiatrist I've been in the fortunate position of speaking with spirits who were possessing my patients. That made me realize that our world is far beyond anything that I had thought possible. My life changed dramatically. I now know that each of us belongs to a world of invisible beings. What a gift that was! Without that awareness I would still believe that you and I belong to a meaningless material community.

Survival is key. Of course, survival after bodily death has been known for millennia. Every religion has said so, though the pictures they give are varied and, in the Western world, scanty. The evidence is available for all to see, although not everyone accepts it. Take it to heart, and it will make all the difference to our lives, because it will affect how we live day by day in our world community. Each one of us has that enormous responsibility.

Thank you for reading my book. Please pass it on.

Afterword

To the Skeptics

This may take some readers by surprise, as I have yet to open a book on psychic research or related matters in which skeptics are welcomed, but since members of the Skeptics Society have made themselves prominent where such matters are discussed, they are admitted here, as an indication of their existence, though not as approval of their message or behavior.

Skepticism began in ancient Greece and covered opinions on virtually every subject. The original Pyrrhonian skeptics argued, justly, that nothing could be certain. Skeptics Society members are strong supporters of today's science. However, they are not scientists, nor are they true skeptics. Members of the Skeptics Society concern themselves only with suppressing what they name "pseudoscience," which means nonphysicalist science.

Why they're so protective of physicalist contemporary science is unclear. Perhaps their motivation relates to their own needs. Their passion for scientific physicalism may be a reaction to early exposure to religious fundamentalism or some other forced belief.

The following is meant for them.

Skeptics Embraced

Skeptics are accepted kindly here!
I too was skeptical once.
No one need fear when like meets like
and truth gives open answers.
That's why I wrote this book. I'm writing this for you.
You're free to ponder every chosen word.

The liveliest questions come from open minds and
*   find the ripening fruit.*
Only clear seeing finds the truest way.
Baseless theory has no future here.
We are the judges
And the time is right for hearts to work together.

Acknowledgments

Acknowledging help received from old and new friends and contacts is one of the special pleasures that comes from writing a book. It's a real joy bringing you all to mind and reliving those creative times.

Senta Frauchiger, although no longer with us, and only a memory to my close family, must come first. Senta, you left this world more than twenty years ago, still uttering your favorite word, "Incredible!" which sprang to the air so joyously, wherever you were. "Incredible!" became more yours with every passing year, as an expression of your joy that our world and its inhabitants could be so beautiful. For those who never met her, I must add that Senta, the gentlest person I ever knew, taught English in a Zurich high school. We shared enthusiasm for English poetry and were in frequent correspondence, Zurich-London-Zurich, for years. Somehow, Senta, you knew my needs before I did. You sent me Sir George Trevelyan's *A Vision of the Aquarian Age* (1977) long before I was ready for it. I was not impressed and told you so, but today, finally, I thank you. "Incredible!"

Lance Trendall set me on the path of treatment by spirit release, which was to help many people, directly or indirectly, overcome the difficulties that had troubled them and sometimes made them seriously ill for years. Lance, I shall always be grateful for your help. I appreciated your generosity in providing me with books by other pioneers in the treatment of spirit attachment and in demonstrating your expertise with my hospital patients.

I am grateful to many others who have influenced my book and helped in more immediate ways. Lois Joy Thurston was the first. Your artistic breath, L-J, was very welcome and got me off to a good start.

Melissa Gilani spent hours and days, at an early stage, in careful reading and suggestions. Thank you, Melissa, for introducing questions that I never thought of asking. Valerie Richards, you too made some helpful comments on the text, for which I am most grateful.

Enthusiasm was vital to buoy me up and keep me writing. That was my life blood. Graham Taylor, an enthusiast from the start, was always helpful with thoughts on publication and ready to lend a hand when text needed shaking. Graham, you even sent an early draft to a top agent, whose reply, thankfully, was unwritten. Fred Zaromba is a name I shall not forget. I am grateful to you, Fred, and to your invisible mum for your great enthusiasm, which I so valued, at an early stage. Edith Fiore, psychologist and explorer in many areas, was more than generous with two published pieces, one a chapter long. I thought I was depending too much on her expertise to ask for a foreword, but I finally succumbed as I knew she would do it brilliantly. She more than fulfilled my hopes. Edee, I count you as an unfailing friend whom I can always turn to. I am much in your debt and am delighted to be sharing these pages with you.

David Lorimer supplied a touch of encyclopedic knowledge that flowed into characteristically helpful comments. Thank you, David. I'm grateful for your interest.

My good friend Tom Zinser allowed me to include details about his guide, Gerod, whose comments nourished an important chapter. Thanks, Tom. That was an important link in the book, and just what I needed. Marcus Scriven (it's great to have a journalist at hand) wielded his textural expertise to perfection. Thanks for that, Marcus. You were busy with film direction, but you made time for me.

I must admit that the book-writing journey has been a bumpy one, especially in the matter of editing, for which I needed and obtained highly expert help at the two-thirds stage from Kasia Trojanowska, on Andrew Powell's recommendation. Though I regarded your changes as final, Kasia, I later made some unexpected changes in content, which turned out to be considerable. The book could not have flowered without your dedication and professional editing. Your hyper-professional views on whether chapters needed to be combined or remodeled and occasionally sacrificed were essential. You made the text stand up, professionally. I shall always be grateful to you. Andrew, your nuggets of advice were a great help to me, and your recommendation was much appreciated.

Dr. Keith Parsons, retired BBC radio producer, has been a most welcome support and contact, since our interest and aims have much in common. We are both trying to bring attractively framed information to large numbers of interested people. For several years, Keith has been providing a wonderful stream of programs with historical accounts of research on survival after death. These are available on YouTube listed under "Documentaries by Dr. Keith Parsons." Material in the programs ranges from mediumship to reincarnation and from the soul leaving the body at death to the awareness and individuality of plants. These programs are works of art. Keith records them in his house or garden, and one has the feeling of being granted a personal interview.

Keith has allowed me to use details from some of his YouTube videos in this book. Keith, it has been wonderful to be able to ask a question and have you come back within minutes with an authoritative answer. Finally, you went carefully through my whole text, making many helpful suggestions. It has been a great pleasure and a real help to engage with you.

Not far from the end, a new figure appeared on the scene, Dr. Wolfgang Spiegel, a family doctor from Vienna. He heard of me from the Nowotny Foundation, which had kindly agreed to let me include a piece from Dr. Karl Nowotny's *Messages from a Doctor in the Fourth Dimension*. Dr. Spiegel took an immediate interest in my book, which he read carefully. Wolfgang, I have greatly appreciated your involvement. We hold very similar views, and I have valued your skill and friendship that have helped in many ways. In particular, you restored the introduction to its original place.

To those who have so kindly written words of appreciation for my book—Dr. Anne Baring, Professor Stafford Betty, Edee Fiore, Ph.D., and Dr. Andrew Powell—thank you; your help has made an important difference.

My thanks to Ian Thorp, of Archive Publishing, who gave me early encouragement and whose use of the word *important* was music to my ears.

Jonathan Beecher, of White Crow Books, played an important part in the publishing journey, and I am most grateful to him for his help and understanding.

Great thanks to Suzanne "Sue" Taylor, from Los Angeles, who worked her magic when it was most required.

Thanks, finally, to the tireless editors Lisa P. Allen and Jill Rogers, who somehow used their skill and great forbearance to see me through my first-time authorship difficulties to reach a satisfactory conclusion. You got me here (not without a phenomenal amount of work), and I'm more than grateful. Lisa, you stayed the whole way, and I have especially appreciated your persistence and clarity of thought that has often found the right solution for difficult sections.

Jeanie Levitan, Editor in Chief, I appreciated your presence, at a difficult time, when your experience was of special value. Manzanita Carpenter, I am most grateful for the marketing abilities that you have exercised so ably.

Richard Grossinger, I so appreciated your welcoming judgment in accepting my book, even though, at the time, it still was far from completion. I am very grateful for your continuing interest and support which brought success.

Writing this book has required knowledge of many scientifically anomalous events to give as full a picture as possible of the relationship of the spiritual dimension and survival. Many of these were not known to me personally, but my aim was to show the wide extent of the subject matter. With so many sources of information to draw on, I am indebted, not only to the publishers, but to the authors and individuals whose stories I have drawn upon. We have been blessed with great teachers. Excerpts are cited verbatim, with the original spelling and punctuation preserved, wherever possible. I have learned much from writing this book and am grateful beyond measure for the spirit guide that has been available with advice on suitability whenever possible.

Notes

REVOLUTIONARY INTRODUCTION

1. The story first appeared in *Proceedings of the Society for Psychical Research*, vol. 11 (1887): 397.

CHAPTER 1.
DYING IN GOOD COMPANY

1. The poem comes from an anthology, *Magic Casements*, by George Trevelyan, who did not know its source or title.
2. William Barrett, *Death-Bed Visions*, 10–11.
3. Fenwick and Fenwick, *Art of Dying*.
4. Karl Nowotny, *Messages from a Doctor in the Fourth Dimension*, vol. 1, 61.

CHAPTER 2.
NEAR-DEATH EXPERIENCE

1. Sartori and Walsh, *Transformative Power of Near-Death Experiences*, 42.
2. Parnia, *What Happens When We Die*, 83.
3. Fenwick and Fenwick, *Truth in the Light*.
4. Van Lommel, Van Wees, Meyers, Elfferich, "Near-Death Experiences in Survivors of Cardiac Arrest."
5. Heim, "Remarks on Fatal Falls, 327–37.
6. Watson, *Romeo Error*, 63.

CHAPTER 4. GENDER DYSPHORIA
RESOLVED BY SPIRIT RELEASE

1. Fiore, *Opening the Closed Door*, 42–50.

CHAPTER 5. A SPIRIT GUIDE ADVISES

1. These excerpts come from an unpublished record of Tom Zinser's first meeting with Gerod.

CHAPTER 7. BELIEF AND KNOWING

1. You can read Crookes's report in Colin Wilson, *After Life.*

CHAPTER 9. REINCARNATION

1. Kean, *Surviving Death,* 36.
2. Fiore, *You Have Been Here Before.*

CHAPTER 10. MESSAGES THROUGH A MEDIUM

1. Dowding, *Lychgate,* 35–37.
2. Taylor, *Witness from Beyond.*
3. Taylor, *Evidence from Beyond,* 80.

CHAPTER 11. HYPNOTIC REGRESSION

1. Newton, *Destiny of Souls,* 307.
2. Newton, *Destiny of Souls,* 317.

CHAPTER 12. MEDIUMSHIP

1. Haraldsson and Matlock, *I Saw a Light and Came Here.*
2. Dowding, *Lychgate,* 105.
3. Dowding, *Lychgate,* 106.
4. Evans, *Billy Grows Up in Spirit.*
5. Wilson, *After Life.*

CHAPTER 13. LISZT, CHOPIN, AND BEETHOVEN INSTRUCT A MEDIUM

1. Brown, *Unfinished Symphonies,* 123.
2. Brown, *Unfinished Symphonies,* 54.
3. Brown, *Unfinished Symphonies,* 138–41.
4. Brown, *Unfinished Symphonies,* 142–48.
5. Brown, *Unfinished Symphonies,* 148–51.
6. Brown, *Immortals at My Elbow.*

CHAPTER 14. HEARING VOICES

1. Gurney, Podmore, and Myers, *Phantasms of the Living*, vol. 1, chapter 20.
2. Caddy, *Flight into Freedom and Beyond*, 53.
3. Van Dusen, *Natural Depth in Man*, 143–60.
4. Nelson, *Healing the Split*, 215.
5. Nelson, *Healing the Split*, 216.

CHAPTER 15. SEEING APPARITIONS

1. Slocum, *Sailing Alone around the World*, 39.
2. Lindbergh, *We*.
3. Myers, *Human Personality and Its Survival of Bodily Death*.
4. *Proceedings of the Society for Psychical Research*, vol. 10 (1916), 380–82.

CHAPTER 16. GUIDING LIGHTS

1. Puhle, *Light Changes*.
2. M. Passy, who had that anecdote from General Rapp himself, related it at the meeting of the Academie des Science Morale et Politiques, April 4, 1846.

CHAPTER 17. TELEPATHY IN HUMANS AND THEIR PETS

1. Myers, *Human Personality and Its Survival of Bodily Death*.

CHAPTER 18. ANIMALS IN THE AFTERLIFE

1. Taylor, *Evidence from Beyond*, 62–63.
2. Vivian, *Doorway*, 61–70.
3. Brown, *Look Beyond Today*, 65.

CHAPTER 19. ASTRAL PROJECTION

1. Myers, *Human Personality and Its Survival of Bodily Death*, 198.
2. Myers, *Human Personality and Its Survival of Bodily Death*, 195.
3. Gregory, *Letters to a Candid Inquirer on Animal Magnetism*.
4. Myers, *Human Personality and Its Survival of Bodily Death*.
5. Myers, *Human Personality and Its Survival of Bodily Death*.

CHAPTER 21. DREAMS

1. Powell, *Hidden Lives of Dreams.*
2. Myers, *Human Personality and Its Survival of Bodily Death,* 107.
3. Gurney, Podmore, and Myers, *Phantasms of the Living,* vol. 1, 338.
4. Roberts, "Deathwalking with Diana."

CHAPTER 22. PREMONITIONS

1. Knight, "The Psychiatrist Who Believed People Could Tell the Future."
2. Van Dusen, *Natural Depth in Man.*
3. Twain, *Autobiography of Mark Twain.*

CHAPTER 23. HEART TRANSPLANTS

1. The childhood cases and others recorded here can be found in Pearsall, Schwartz, and Russek, "Changes in Heart Transplant Recipients That Parallel the Personalities of Their Donors."

CHAPTER 24. ENERGY HEALING

1. This account comes from Sebastian's treatment report. I have also been in touch with Anne, Mona's mother, who was happy for me to report her account here.
2. Bengston and Krinsley, "The Effect of the 'Laying on of Hands' on Transplanted Breast Cancer in Mice."

Glossary

afterlife/interlife. Can be either existence between lives, for those who believe in reincarnation, or existence before and after the one and only earth life, for those who believe in one life only. *Interlife* has reincarnation implied or confirmed.

astral projection. The ability to project one's awareness beyond normal perceptual limits. Also known as out-of-body experience (OBE).

brownie. For chocolate eaters. Actually, a Scottish spirit who cleans the house and tends the garden at night while residents are asleep.

clairvoyance. The knowledge of worldly and perhaps otherworldly things that surpasses the ordinary limits of perception.

consciousness. The subjective awareness of what is happening in and around one. The word is being given an ever wider use.

consensual hallucination. An awareness that includes more than one person—for instance, when two people experience the same hallucination.

drop-in communicator. A previously unknown spirit of a deceased person who communicates with members of a spirit rescue circle.

end-of-life experience. An experience of a dying person that is beyond ordinary perception.

entity. A word sometimes used to indicate a spiritual being.

higher self. A part of the soul that has a deep knowledge of the incarnate soul and can be a useful co-therapist. (Note: *Higher self* is variously used by different writers. I have taken the definition given in Katherine Mackey's book *Soul Awareness: A Guide's Message,* which is used in Thomas Zinser's *Soul-Centered Healing.*)

incubus. A male spirit that sexually attacks a woman while she is sleeping. The woman's experience of the incubus is considered psychotic or delusional by psychiatry, doubtless because it seems impossible by current beliefs.

Light. When written with a capital letter, *Light* is used to mean the enlightened spiritual presence. It may also be used to indicate God.

materialism. See *physicalism*.

medium. An individual who is aware of the spirits of the deceased and usually works with a spirit guide.

mesmerism. A healing technique developed by Franz Mesmer, the success of which he originally attributed to his use of magnets. Mesmerism was later termed hypnotism by James Braid, who used a verbal induction.

near-death experience. An experience often, but not invariably, associated with a critical state in which death is thought to have taken place. The individual is aware of various experiences such as being above the body, watching attempts at resuscitation, and passing down a tunnel to a bright light, where they are met by divine beings or deceased relatives who tell them that they should return to the physical body. Afterward it is common to lose a fear of death.

Ouija board. A board with letters and numbers used to communicate with spirits.

out-of-body experience (OBE). A state in which one's awareness travels beyond the physical body. While it is commonly a part of the near-death experience, it may also occur unintentionally, without an obvious stimulus (see Robert Monroe in chapter 20).

physicalism. The predominant philosophy of the Western world, on which most of contemporary science is built, that postulates that the universe is made of matter and that the brain creates consciousness.

psychokinesis. The ability to influence, by intention only, the state of material objects and changes in electrical activity during research.

remote viewing. The astral body travels away from the physical body to gain information about areas out of sight. This can be induced intentionally for espionage.

rescue circle. Two or more people working together with the intention of connecting with those who have died to help them move into the spirit world proper for communication. There will be at least one spirit medium in the rescue circle.

revelation. A religious term for disclosing some form of truth or knowledge through communication with a deity or supernatural entity. When a religious figure, such as Christ or Mohammed, hears a hallucinatory voice, it is known as a revelation because it is said to be information from God.

Rorschach test. A psychological test in which the patient is asked to interpret an image produced by a series of inkblots.

Spiritism. A philosophical, spiritual system of psychotherapy, developed by Allan Kardec, along nonmaterial, scientific lines and based on information obtained from spirits communicating through mediums. Reincarnation is an essential aspect of Spiritism, which contrasts strongly from Spiritualism for this reason.

Spiritualism. A religion and healing practice based on knowledge of spiritual activity as obtained from mediumistic activity stimulated by the Fox sisters' mediumship of the 1850s.

table tapping. An activity where a group of people sit around a table with palms up. The spirits communicate by lifting the table a little off the ground.

telepathy. The transfer of ideas and sensations from one mind to another without the agency of the recognized sense organs.

veridical. Truthful. A term used when confirming the reality of an experience that might otherwise be dismissed as imaginary or delusional.

Recommended Reading and Viewing

All of these resources are beautifully written and highly original.

Baring, Anne. *Dream of the Cosmos*. 2nd ed. Archive Publishing, 2020. A deep and passionate history of humanity, explaining how femininity and our spiritual nature have been suppressed and separated from the world soul, pointing the way to recovery. The story is intimately, brilliantly told.

Crabtree, Adam. *Multiple Man*. London: Grafton Books, 1988. Finely drawn history of hypnosis (especially magnetism). Also, multiple personality and possession. Highly recommended.

Fiore, Edith. *Opening the Closed Door: A Psychologist Shares Four Fascinating Cases*. Self-published, 2019. Fiore give masterly presentation of clinical skills in chapters 4 (Spirit Release) and 9 (Regression for Reincarnation).

Gober, Mark. *An End to Upside Down Thinking*. Waterside Press, 2018. Well-drawn analysis of the present state of scientific thinking and the need for change as we approach a revolution in our perception of consciousness. Mark gives a great, complete and persuasive presentation. Highly energized.

Kean, Leslie. *Surviving Death*. New York: Penguin Random House, 2017. The best presentation yet of the case for survival. The book contains many well-written accounts by experts in their specialties. Kean gives compelling well-researched case studies, some of them from her own friends and family. Convincingly told.

Mayer, Elizabeth Lloyd. *Extraordinary Knowing*. New York: Bantam, 2008. Lisby, as she was universally known, on recovering her daughter's stolen cello through a professional dowser, devotes her highly successful career as psychoanalyst to investigating the claims of many others whose lives are devoted to the study of anomalous experiences. Lisby uses her great intelligence to study the paranormal. She is a fascinating writer, whose book will hold your attention better than any murder mystery.

Parsons, Keith. (See essential entry in Acknowledgments.)

Powell, Andrew. *Conversations with the Soul: A Psychiatrist Reflects; Essays on Life, Death, and Beyond.* London: Muswell Hill Press, 2018. Anne Baring writes the foreword to the 2017 volume.

———. *The Ways of the Soul: A Psychiatrist Reflects; Essays on Life, Death, and Beyond.* London: Muswell Hill Press, 2017. Andrew Powell's books are in a class of their own. I recommend them highly for their intellectual brilliance and solid understanding of both transpersonal psychiatry, as promoted by C. G. Jung and S. Grof, and the quantum physics connection with psychotherapy. The books show excellent examples of Andrew Powell's clinical work and will be of great interest to workers in this area. The wording and thinking are not abstruse and can be readily followed.

Wilson, Colin. *After Life: Survival of the Soul.* 2nd ed. Woodbury, Minn.: Llewellyn Publications, 2000. Colin Wilson put a lifetime's experience and study into this book. He writes well and his style is convincing. A highly enjoyable and persuasive read.

Zinser, Thomas. *Soul-Centered Healing: A Psychologist's Extraordinary Journey into the Realms of Sub-Personalities, Spirits, and Past Lives.* Grand Rapids, Mich.: Union Street Press, 2010. Tom's first book is well planned and well written. Having discovered a spirit guide, he made good use of the good fortune and they met weekly for twenty years, during which Tom learned a vast amount the inner workings of the mind, both ego states and intruding spirits. As a result, he is now teaching worldwide. His findings are revolutionary.

Bibliography

Achterberg, Jeanne, et al. "Evidence for Correlations between Distant Intentionality and Brain Function in a Functional Magnetic Resonance Imaging Analysis." *Journal of Alternative and Complementary Medicine* 11, no. 6 (2005): 965–71.

Banks, Frances. *Frontiers of Revelation: An Empirical Study in the Psychology of Psychic and Spiritual Experience.* London: Max Parrish, 1962.

Barrett, William. *Death-Bed Visions.* London: Methuen & Co., 1926; reprint, Wellingborough, U.K.: Aquarian Press, 1986.

Bengston, William F., and David Krinsley. "The Effect of the 'Laying on of Hands' on Transplanted Breast Cancer in Mice." *Journal of Scientific Exploration* 14, no. 3(2000).

Benson, Robert Hugh. *Life after Death in the Worlds Unseen.* Published in 1953. Available on the New Earth: Earth Changes and the Ascension of Planet Earth website.

Betty, Stafford. *The Afterlife Unveiled.* Winchester, U.K.: O-Books, 2010.

———. *When Did You Ever Become Less by Dying?* Guildford, Surrey, U.K.: White Crow Books, 2016.

Brown, Rosemary. *Immortals at My Elbow.* Melbourne: Hill of Content Publishing Co., 1975.

———. *Look beyond Today.* New York: Transworld Publishers, 1986.

———. *Unfinished Symphonies.* London: Souvenir Press, 1971.

Brunton, Paul. *A Search in Secret Egypt.* London, U.K.: Rider & Co., 1938.

Caddy, Eileen. *Flight into Freedom and Beyond.* Forres, U.K.: Findhorn Press, 2002.

Dossey, Larry. *Healing Beyond the Body: Medicine and the Infinite Reach of the Mind.* Boston: Shambhala, 2003.

Dowding, Hugh. *Lychgate: The Entrance to the Path*. London: Rider and Company, 1945.

Dunne, J. W. *An Experiment with Time*. Newburyport, Mass.: Hampton Roads Publishing, 2001.

Evans, Michael. *Billy Grows Up in Spirit: A Cockney Lad Returns after Death to Tell His Story*. Exeter, U.K.: Whole Being Centre Publications, 1997.

Fenwick, Peter, and Elizabeth Fenwick. *The Art of Dying*. London: Continuum, 2008.

———. *The Truth in the Light*. Guildford, U.K.: White Crow Books, 1996.

Fiore, Edith. *Opening the Closed Door: A Psychologist Shares Four Fascinating Cases*. Self-published, 2019.

———. *The Unquiet Dead: A Psychologist Treats Spirit Possession*. New York: Ballantine Books, 1987.

———. *You Have Been Here Before: A Psychologist Looks at Past Lives*. New York: Ballantine Books, 1978.

Fontana, David. *Is There an Afterlife?* Winchester, U.K.: O-Books, 2005.

Foos-Graber, Anya. *Deathing: An Intelligent Alternative for the Final Moments of Life*. Newburyport, Mass.: Nicolas-Hays, 1989.

Gallup, G. *The Gallup Poll: Public Opinion 1991*. Washington, D.C.: Scholarly Resources, 1992.

Greaves, Helen. *Testimony of Light: An Extraordinary Message of Life after Death*. London: Rider, 2005.

Gregory, William. *Letters to a Candid Inquirer on Animal Magnetism*. London: Taylor, Walton, and Maberly, 1851.

Grosso, Michael. *The Man Who Could Fly*. Lanham: Md.: Rowman & Littlefield, 2016.

Gurney, Edmund, Frank Podmore, and Frederic W. H. Myers. *Phantasms of the Living*, 2 vols. London: Trubner & Co. Ludgate Hill, 1886.

Haraldsson, Erlendur, and Matlock, James. *I Saw a Light and Came Here*. Guildford, Surrey, U.K.: White Crow Books, 2016.

Harvey, William. *An Anatomical Exercise Concerning the Motion of the Heart and Blood in Animals*. Translated by Robert Willis. U.K.: J. M. Dent & Co., 1906.

Heim, Albert. "Remarks on Fatal Falls" ("Notizen uber den Tod durch absturz"). *Jahrbuch des Schweizer Alpenclub*, 1892.

Holzer, Hans. *The Psychic Side of Dreams*. New York: Doubleday, 1976.

Jacobsen, Annie. *Phenomena: The Secret History of the U.S. Government's*

Investigations into Extrasensory Perception and Psychokinesis. New York: Little, Brown and Company, 2017.

Jung, Carl G. *Memories, Dreams, Reflections*. New York: Fontana Press, 1995.

Kean, Leslie. *Surviving Death*. New York: Penguin Random House, 2017.

———. *UFOs: Generals, Pilots, and Government Officials Go on the Record*. New York: Three Rivers Press, 2010.

Knight, Sam. "The Psychiatrist Who Believed People Could Tell the Future." *New Yorker* website, February 25, 2019.

Kuhn, Thomas. *The Structure of Scientific Revolutions*. Chicago: University of Chicago Press, 1963.

Lindbergh, Charles. *We*. New York: G. P. Putnam's Sons, 1927.

Mackey, Katherine. *Soul Awareness: A Guide's Message*. Self-published, 2012.

Maeterlinck, Maurice. *The Unknown Guest*. London: Methuen & Co., 1914.

Mayer, Elizabeth Lloyd. *Extraordinary Knowing*. New York: Bantam, 2008.

Miller, Judith. *Healing the Western Soul*. St. Paul, Minn.: Paragon House, 2015.

Milton, Richard. *Forbidden Science*. London: Fourth Estate Ltd., 1994.

Monroe, Robert A. *Journeys Out of the Body*. New York: Doubleday Anchor, 1971.

———. *Ultimate Journey*. New York: First Main Street Books, 1996.

Moody, Raymond A. *Life after Life*. San Francisco: HarperOne, 2001.

Myers, F. W. H. *Human Personality and Its Survival of Bodily Death*. Mineola, N.Y.: Dover Publications, 2005.

Nelson, John. *Healing the Split*. Albany: State University of New York Press, 1990.

Newton, Michael. *Destiny of Souls*. Woodbury, Minn.: Llewellyn Publications, 2000.

Nowotny, Karl. *Messages from a Doctor in the Fourth Dimension*, vol. 1 of 6. First published under the title *Mediale Schriften*, Germany 1972. English edition Bristol, U.K.: Longdunn Press Ltd., 1996.

Parnia, Sam. *What Happens When We Die*. Carlsbad, Calif.: Hay House, 2005.

Parrott, Ian. *The Music of Rosemary Brown*. Buntingford, U.K.: Regency Press, 1978.

Pearsall, Paul. *The Heart's Code*. New York: Broadway, 1999.

Pearsall, Paul, Gary Schwartz, and Linda Russek. "Changes in Heart Transplant Recipients That Parallel the Personalities of Their Donors." *Integrative Medicine* 2, nos. 2/3 (1999): 65–72.

Powell, Melinda. *The Hidden Lives of Dreams*. London: Bonnier Books, 2020.

Puhle, Annekatrin. *Light Changes*. Guildford, U.K.: White Crow Books, 2013.

Rhine, Joseph Banks. *Extra-Sensory Perception*. Boston: Boston Society for Psychic Research, 1934.

Ritchie, George G. *Return from Tomorrow*. Ada, Mich.: Fleming H. Revell Co., 1978.

Roberts, Maureen. "Deathwalking with Diana: Shamanic Dreams and Visions of a Resurrected Grail Myth." Jung Circle website, 1998.

Robertson, Tricia. *Things You Can Do When You're Dead*. London: Waterstones, 2013.

Russell, Ronald. *The Journey of Robert Monroe: From Out-of-Body Explorer to Consciousness Pioneer*. Newburyport, Mass.: Hampton Roads Publishing, 2007.

Sartori, Penny, and Kelly Walsh. *The Transformative Power of Near-Death Experiences*. London: Watkins Media, 2017.

Slocum, Joshua. *Sailing Alone around the World*. New York: Century Company, 1900.

Sylvia, Claire. *A Change of Heart*. New York: Little, Brown and Company, 1997.

Taylor, Ruth Mattson, ed. *Evidence from Beyond*. New York: Brett Books, Inc., 1999.

———, ed. *Witness from Beyond*. South Portland, Maine: Foreword Books, 1980.

Trevelyan, George. *Magic Casements: The Use of Poetry in the Expanding of Consciousness*. U.K.: Gateway, 1996.

Twain, Mark. *Autobiography of Mark Twain*. San Francisco: Harper, 2000.

Van Dusen, Wilson. *The Natural Depth in Man*. West Chester, Pa.: Swedenborg Foundation, 1981.

Van Lommel P., R. Van Wees, V. Meyers, and I. Elfferich. "Near-Death Experiences in Survivors of Cardiac Arrest: A Prospective Study in the Netherlands." *Lancet* 358 (2001): 2039–45.

Vivian, Margaret. *The Doorway*. London: Psychic Press, 1941.

Volgyesi, Ferenc Andras. *Hypnosis of Man and Animals*. New York: Bailliere, Tindall & Cassell, 1966.

Watson, Lyall. *The Romeo Error*. London: Hodder and Stoughton Ltd., 1974.

Wickland, Carl. *Thirty Years among the Dead*. London: Spiritualist Press, 1974.

Wilson, Colin. *After Life: Survival of the Soul*. 2nd ed. Woodbury, Minn.: Llewellyn Publication, 2000.

Zinser, Thomas. *The Practice of Soul-Centered Healing*, vol. 1. Grand Rapids, Mich.: Union Street Press, 2013.

———. *Soul-Centered Healing*. Grand Rapids, Mich.: Union Street Press, 2010.

Zohar, Danah. *Through the Time Barrier: A Study of Precognition and Modern Physics*. London: Heinemann, 1983.

List of Accounts

CHAPTER 12. MEDIUMSHIP

CHAPTER 13. LISZT, CHOPIN, AND BEETHOVEN INSTRUCT A MEDIUM

CHAPTER 14. HEARING VOICES

CHAPTER 15. SEEING APPARITIONS

CHAPTER 22. PREMONITIONS

CHAPTER 23. HEART TRANSPLANTS

CHAPTER 24. ENERGY HEALING

Index